Easy-to-Sew Playful Toys

Debra Quartermain

©2004 Debra Quartermain
Published by

kp books
An imprint of F+W Publications, Inc.

700 East State Street • Iola, WI 54990-0001
715-445-2214 • 888-457-2873

Our toll-free number to place an order or obtain
a free catalog is (800) 258-0929.

Library of Congress Catalog Number: 2004093894

ISBN: 0-87349-838-0

Edited by Maria L. Turner
Designed by Kara Grundman

Printed in the United States of America

Acknowledgments

Long, long ago—well, perhaps not that long ago but definitely far away—a young girl dreamed of creating and writing books. It may have taken a few years, but the dream became a reality. I have to thank my "fairy godmother," Julie Stephani, for believing in me and starting the dream. The rest of the dream came true in a quiet little place in Wisconsin, the home of KP Books. The days I spent there for the photo shoot were wonderful. From the moment I was picked up at the airport by Jerry, I felt at home. My editor, Maria Turner, and I worked together like we had been doing it for years. The other editors and staff were so very friendly, taking time to keep me entertained and well-fed!

The pure joy of the book was the photo shoot where Bob Best photographed the kids playing with all the toys: Abbie, Logan, Charlie, Megan, Vanessa, Dylan, Jared, and mom Corinne. There was singing, dancing, lots of jokes, and laughter. The spirit of the toys was captured perfectly.

Back at home, Charles Bliss illustrated all my rough drawings transforming them with his magic wand. My amazing artist friend Deborah Peyton took my animals and brought them to life with her whimsical drawings. Working with her was pure inspiration and from this collaboration a partnership was born. Maria and my talented designer, Kara Grundman, then put it all together and the magic happened.

Thank you to David Fones from Daisy Kingdom, Donna Robertson, Fran Morgan from Fabric Café, and Funky Fibers for their generosity. I'm further grateful to Sew n' Sew for allowing us to borrow a sewing machine for photography purposes.

As always, thanks also to my dearest friends (Donna, Lorine, Sharon, Karen, and Alison), my family (Bob, my mom, and my lovely daughters Amanda and Kate), and the many delightful children in my life who have made this book possible. Their encouragement is strong and constant giving me the gift to dream, to believe. Yes, dreams do come true; mine truly have.

My biggest dream is for this book to reach many children and touch their lives with love and laughter. Every child needs a cuddly playful friend created with love.

Vanessa was among the many child models who not only had fun with the toys, but also helped bring author Debra Quartermain's dream to fruition.

Table of Contents

Introduction 6

Chapter 1: The Fun Starts Here 8

Once Upon a Time 10

Playing Safe 10

It's Tool Time! 11

Material Matters 12

Accessorize! 14

Drawing and Sewing Patterns 15

Attach, Patch, Latch 16

Heads or Tails 17

Friendly Faces 18

Spots and Dots 19

Pockets Full of Fun 20

All Together Now 21

Chapter 2: Purrfect Pals and GRReat Buds 22

Hot Dawg 24

PeeWee Pup 28

Catastrophe 31

Polkadilly Pooch 36

Skittles the Kitten 40

Chapter 3: Wiggles, Jiggles, and Lots of Giggles 46

Wacky Wilma 48

Oh Ladybug 53

Fred Frog 56

Tuttles Turtle 60

Butterfly Flower 64

Chapter 4: Puppets and Poppets 68

Bumbles Bunny 70

Leonardo Lion 75

Hamlet Hamster 79

Hocus P. Ocus 83

Marvin Monkey 86

Chapter 5: Topsy-Turvy and A Little Groovy...................92

Willy Nilly..94

Hairy-Etta..97

Geeker..102

Raggle Taggle.....................................105

Pencil Poppers...................................108

Chapter 6: Bears, Hares, and Hugs to Share.................110

Ted ZZZ Bear....................................112

Wibbit Wabbit...................................116

Dudz Bear...120

Wibbles..125

Glam Bear..129

More Creative Play...........................134

Stories and Ideas..............................135

Lights, Laughter, Action..................137

Pattern Sheets Index and Project Numbers..............140

Source Information.........................142

About the Author..................143

Introduction

The soft toys in this book are sewn from brightly colored fabrics with button eyes and felt noses. Each basic pattern is the same as the pieces are cut and assembled. As the toy nears completion, it resembles very much the pattern, but there is a difference—slight but detectable. Loving hands fill each toy, adding hopes, dreams, and wishes. As the eyes are sewn and noses added, the personality is born.

The toy is given in love and received with love. The child who receives this wonderful toy continues the journey and makes the toy a real friend and playmate.

These soft toys all have a story to tell, stories of playful times, quiet confidences, and loving cuddles. Each toy is ready to play games anytime, anywhere. Favorite games of dominoes, ring toss, and tic-tac-toe are built into these colorful, creative, and happy toys. Play is the delightful work of children. Through play, children develop imagination, coordination, and identity.

Come inside to a playground filled with polka-dotted dogs and purple cats, wacky birds and wild things. They are so easy to sew, so easy to love, so easy to give. Share some fun with a special child by creating together some of the smaller toys found within. Creative hands fill hearts with joy and the air with laughter.

Creating each playful friend for the first time made me smile. This is the gift I wish to give to all of you—a smile from the heart.

chapter 1

THE FUN STARTS HERE

The fun definitely starts here with all kinds of great tips, information, and techniques to easily make creative, playful toys. Everything is fully explained from choosing fabric to applying the last spot. Come discover the fun and choose a furry, fuzzy friend to create—or make two or three! My sewing area looks like a polka-dot pound filled with colorful four-legged friends. Right now, there is a bright red dog hanging over my sewing machine. I don't have the heart to tell him he can't sew or read the book.

Once Upon a Time ...

There was a little girl who made dolls and toys from fabric scraps on a miniature sewing machine. She watched her mother transform worn drapes and outgrown clothes into matching outfits for them both. As the girl grew up, sewing clothing and soft toys were part of her life.

Many years passed, and the little girl had two precious daughters of her own. Each wore handmade outfits, from tiny shoes to the precious bonnets. Soft, cuddly toys filled their rooms. Everywhere, there were lovingly sewn treasures.

The daughters, of course, are mine. I made them soft toys and dolls and watched them play with delight. Their favorites held a surprise, like a carrot bag with bunnies inside or a pop-up puppet. As they grew older, birthday parties and class projects were creative events where everyone got to make an easy toy. Creating for and with children is such a rewarding experience, watching their imagination soar and the joy they experience in mastering new skills.

Now in this book, all of those memorable times are captured in these playful toys that are full of surprises and fun. Please share these toys with the children in your lives. A delightful time awaits you.

Playing Safe

The first concern with any toy is safety and age suitability. Manufactured toys must conform to certain regulations by law. The same considerations must be made for handmade toys for children. The soft toys in this book are for children older than three, who are past the age of putting toy parts in their mouths and are no longer in danger of swallowing small pieces.

Other safety issues to consider include making sure fabrics are of good quality and prewashed to remove any sizing or residue. Stuffing materials should be washable, polyester fiberfill only. Use safety eyes in the toys for the younger children. Buttons and other decorative items should be attached very securely. Upholstery thread is used throughout the book for its super strength in attaching buttons as well as arms, legs, tails, and heads. All seams are sewn twice for extra durability. The larger, softer animals are wonderful for the younger children (4 to 7 years old). The smaller toys with small parts are appropriate for those children 6 to 10 years old.

In each chapter, there is one toy that is an easy project parents and children can make together. Safety here is also very important when children are working with sharp scissors and needles. For younger children, I suggest cutting out pieces for them and giving them a short embroidery needle to work with. Constant supervision is important. Having their needle double-threaded and knotted will make sewing easier and keep the needle visible. Make sure needles are placed in a pin cushion when not being used. Rotary cutters and irons should not be used when creating a toy with children.

Older children can use sharp scissors and longer needles, but adult supervision is also necessary and part of the fun. Teaching children how to use the tools properly and safely while creating a fun toy introduces them to the wonderful world of sewing.

Safety is important, regardless of the age of the child. Small toys, like Hocus P. Ocus, shown above with Logan, should be made for children who are at least 6 years old.

It's Tool Time!

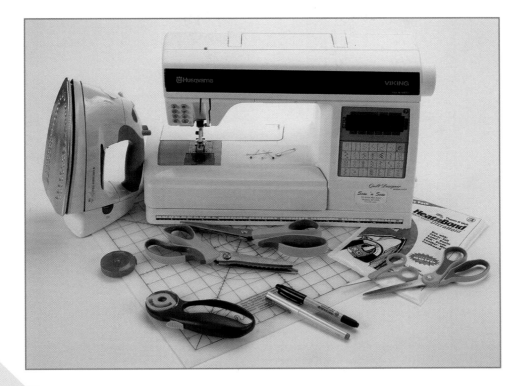

With the useful and extensive number of tools available, sewing today is truly a joy.

For the projects in this book, a good, basic machine is all that is needed. A straight, zigzag, and buttonhole stitch are the only stitches required for these toys. A Teflon® presser foot is excellent for guiding heavier fabrics through the machine. Sewing with heavier-weight fabrics, such as fleece and fun furs, is easier with a good machine. If you plan to sew with these materials often and are looking for a new machine, inform the dealer of your requirements.

Some of my favorite tools are made by Fiskars: a ruler, cutting mat, rotary cutter, and scissors. Scallop-edged scissors create decorative edges on several of the toys.

An iron, measuring tape, pins, and needles are also required. For pins, I prefer the long quilters' pins with the colored heads. They are easy to pull in and out, plus the contrasting colors show up well against the fabrics. There are several types of needles I will suggest for these projects. First, sewing machine needles that work well with fleece are a universal 70 or 80 needle. Soft sculpture needles from 3.5" to 7" in length are useful in adding eye beads or other features that require passing through stuffed heads or body parts. For the toys in this book, a 4" or 5" needle is the longest you will need. Size 22 embroidery needles are good for small features and for larger faces. I often use the 3.5" sculpture needle.

Disappearing marker, a black fine-point marker, and chalk are useful in drawing patterns and marking features for sewing.

Besides the tools needed, there are other elements to be considered before beginning a project. Good lighting is needed, especially if you are young at heart, but your eyes are a little more mature.

Set aside some space specifically for sewing and crafting that is bright and cheery with a good-sized worktable. Decorate with your favorite things and add some whimsical sewing-related accessories. If you are creating wonderful projects, you should be surrounded by an inspiring and nurturing atmosphere.

Material Matters

Walking into a fabric store is like the candy store of dreams, or almost. I do admit to the occasional craving for chocolate, which my local fabric store does not sell. Everything else I could want in fabric selection though is there. In sewing for children, durability and safety are issues to consider. Fabrics with softness and texture and washability should be used. I always wash all fabrics used in kids' projects before sewing with them.

Working with Polar Fleece

Polar fleece is one of the best materials to use in kids' sewing. It comes in a vast array of lively colors, is easy to sew with, and is very soft and cuddly. There are many types and quality ranges of fleece available. A medium-weight fleece with a non-pill finish is excellent. Sometimes, it is difficult to tell the right side of fleece. By pulling along the selvage edge, you will find that it will curl to the right side. These toys are handled a lot, so use good-quality fleece. Fleece has a stretch, which gives the features more expression as you sculpt with it.

When stuffing polar fleece toys, use small amounts of fiberfill, being sure to push it into the curves. Because of the fabric's stretch, it is easy to keep stuffing, but you want the toy to be soft. Stuff enough so that the shape is filled out, but the fabric is not stretched. Once the toy is completely filled with fiberfill, just press it between your hands to smooth out any possible lumps. Some of the toys do need firmer parts, which are usually small elements of their construction. The instructions will specifically state which parts to stuff firmer.

When sewing fleece to other fabrics, place the fleece on top.

I find it is easier to sew with the firmer fabric on the bottom.

There are also several other stretch materials similar to fleece, like velour, terry, or fuzzy knits, that add even more texture to children's toys. All should be treated the same way as fleece.

Fun Fur and Felt Tips

There are many synthetic fun furs available. Most fabric stores carry a few, and the colors are vibrant.
The texture of fur is appealing to everyone—so soft and cuddly. Fun fur is easy to work with and gives great results. It, too, has some stretch, which I like in the shaping of faces and bodies.

Fur has a nap. When using any type of fabric with a nap, determine the nap by running your hand over it. For most projects, the nap should run down the body. Just like when you pet your cat, it wouldn't be as soothing to pat if the fur was going the opposite direction your hand was going. When working with fur, always cut through the back only, not the fur fibers, with sharp scissors taking short little cuts.

Felt is a staple in making toys. It is so easy to sew with, and the colors are wonderful. The glitter felts will certainly be a hit with the kids. I used glitter felt for Hocus P. Ocus's wizard hat.

Plush felt, like fur, also has a nap, so determine that first with your hand before laying out pattern pieces. Fabric glue bonds well with the felt. Combining different materials with their varying textures really adds to the charm of the toys. For those special touches of color, gorgeous ribbons add the final detail.
There are many fun patterns, and the quality makes them very durable.

Getting Attached

Thread is a basic element in keeping the toys together. It needs to be durable and the best quality. Sewing and embroidery threads are two items I couldn't work without. Upholstery thread is my favorite for a super-strong thread. I use it extensively throughout the book. Synthetic thread works best for sewing fleece. Embroidery floss is smooth and has a slight sheen, which brings mouths to life.

For attaching some features, use Fabri-Tac™. It dries quickly and gives a superior bond. It's excellent for all those felt noses in your future. It does have a slight odor when using it, but dries clear and odorless.

Filled with Fun

For filling these soft cuddly toys, quality polyester fiberfill is a must. I have tried several brands and really do not have a favorite; several brands of good-quality fiberfills are readily available in sewing and department stores. A product that has softness and does not clump produces a superior toy. Allergies are something that many children do have, so high-quality stuffing materials are extremely necessary. Of course, the huggable factor is of utmost importance.

Plastic doll pellets are good for small toys like the beanbag bugs in the Fred Frog game, where just a loose shape with some weight is needed.

Most of the products used for these toys are well-known brand items that should be available at your local fabric, craft, or quilt shop. Specific fabric choices shown in the projects are to serve as a guide. Choose the bright fabrics that appeal to you when making the projects. If you cannot find a certain item, please refer to the source list at the back of the book.

Hamlet Hamster's head/body is stuffed with polyester fiberfill to give the toy its shape and plush feel.

Accessorize!

Sewing and creating is so exciting today. There is no end to the fabulous products to use. I was very lucky to be able to do a book where I could use a wide array of accessories to create the toys. The details add personality-plus to the toys.

Since I have daughters, hair accessories have been a staple in our home. Even though they are older, they still both like fun hair elastics and clips. I wanted to make some kind of wild hairdos on a couple of the toys, so I visited the local department store hair product aisle. Wow! What great finds there are there: fuzzy chenille elastics with sparkly flowers, bugs, and bold colors. I brought a few different packages home, and since they were inexpensive, that was an even extra bonus. Actually, the idea for Hairy-Etta, the topsy-turvy doll, came from the wonderful hair accessories. With their bright colors and stretch, I used them for collars and clothing trims, too.

Connect-It!™ no-sew reversible craft squares and the products to put them together (Button-It!™ and Lace-It!™) inspired a couple of easy toys like Leonardo Lion.

With Leonardo, I also used two other new finds. Cozy chenille strips added great textured grass to Leonardo's hideout and for his mane, I used some cool sparkly fibers.

Of course, there are all the vast array of decorative trims and buttons to choose from. Buttons in every shape and color are such fun to add. When adding any trim, consider its placement, especially if it is on a bedtime toy. They shouldn't be in a location where they will irritate the child. Also take into consideration the age of the child. The fun part is there are many places for these fun trims.

Before starting a project just walk the aisles at your fabric store. Look at everything. Spark your creativity by feeding your senses. I truly believe that from the beginning of any project, your positive energy is crucial. The expression of the toy will come alive when it is created with a joyful heart.

Hairy-Etta was inspired by the wide array of hair accessories for girls.

Drawing and Sewing Patterns

There are often several ways to do certain techniques, especially in creative techniques; we find a way that works best for us. I use a couple of techniques for drawing and sewing patterns, depending on the fabric or size of pattern piece. To fit all the pattern pieces on the pattern sheets, many of the pieces are marked to cut on the fold. This can be handled two ways. First, fold over the fabric at one end to fit the piece on, pin the piece to it, and cut it out. The second way is my preferred way of doing it, and I think the easiest. Take a piece of lightweight cardboard that is twice the size of the pattern piece. Cut out the pattern piece and glue it to one side of the cardboard. Fold the cardboard in half and cut around to make a full pattern piece. The pieces are now ready to draw around or pin to the fabrics.

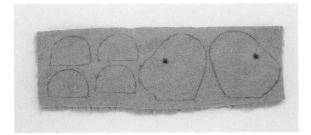

A Sharpie marker or disappearing marker is perfect for drawing around pattern pieces, as shown here.

These techniques described are for the initial pattern sewing. A Sharpie marker or disappearing marker is perfect for drawing around the pattern pieces. For fur, it is necessary to draw the pieces individually. Sometimes, it is also easier to draw around a pattern piece on a larger piece of fabric. I must admit, when the fabric moves a little, I have gone off the edge and missed the seam. I draw around a pattern piece and then sew it as often as I can. For smaller pieces, especially when you are sewing completely around them, I find it easier to draw around one pattern piece and then cut it out. Place it on top of a piece of fabric slightly larger, pin, sew, and cut out. This is especially good for felt.

The other option is pinning and cutting out. Throughout the book I use all of these techniques. Find out what works best for you. Only use the Sharpie on heavier fabrics. Make sure to cut the black line off. On other fabrics, use the disappearing marker, as long as you are sewing the pieces right away. For very dark fabrics, chalk is a good choice for drawing pattern pieces.

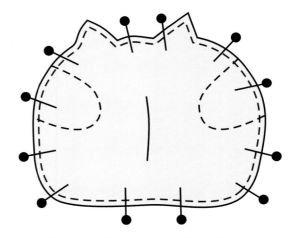

Good pinning ensures the pieces stay together while you sew.

Once construction of the toy is under way, good pinning ensures the pieces will all stay together while you sew, especially when there are other body pieces to catch in between. It is easier if you pin the pieces together and sew from the center point on curved pieces down each side.

When sewing seams on fun furs, make sure to tuck the fur inside first as you pin. If any fur does become caught in the seams, use a needle to pull it out.

Sew seams in the same direction, beginning at the center point on rounded pieces and at the top on straight pieces. This prevents distortion of the piece or features. I recommend this for any of the materials used in the book.

If you find the pieces are bulky and you prefer not to pin and sew, then baste the pieces together with large stitches and a contrasting thread.

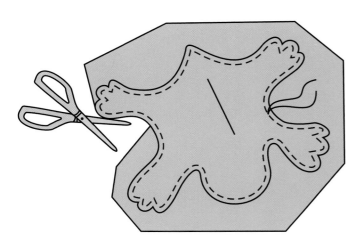

After cutting out one pattern piece, place it on a slightly larger piece of fabric and pin in place. Then, sew and cut it out.

Attach, Patch, Latch

This illustration shows Polkadilly's legs being attached with upholstery thread. The legs are inserted into the body and small stitches, through all layers, hold each leg in place. Repeat the stitching.

One of the best parts of sewing with all of these fuzzy, soft materials is the forgiving nature of them. Stitches are almost invisible.

Securely attaching all pieces is absolutely necessary for all toy parts. Hot Dawg, in particular, has dangly limbs that kids are going to grab. Toys are meant to be handled and therefore need to be put together solidly. I use upholstery thread extensively to hand-sew on body parts, as shown in the illustration above. Use small stitches and go over the stitches a second time to reinforce. Cut the thread in a 2-foot length and insert it through the needle. Most often, instead of a knot at the end, I like to take several small stitches on top of each other to secure the thread and do so at the end of stitching also.

The materials in the book, like the fleece and furs, allow the stitches to sink in, making them invisible, especially when they are small. To add separate body parts, which are often stuffed, attach them with upholstery thread.

There are also many body openings on the toys that need to be sewn shut. Many of the patterns are sewn completely around on the seams and a slit is cut to turn them through in the center. This method gives the body an even shape because I find that sometimes it is difficult to unnoticeably sew an opening on the seam shut when it is on a curve. Most of the slits are hidden by other pieces or on the bottom. Due to the forgiving nature of fleece and furs, the stitches again disappear.

To sew an opening shut using the ladder stitch:

1 Begin at one end with the stitches secure.

2 Take small stitches back and forth from one side of the body to the other, catching the edge of the slit with the needle, as shown in the illustration at the top of the second column.

3 Pull the stitches tight, and they disappear.

4 Secure the thread at the other end.

Sew an opening shut by taking small stitches back and forth from one side of the body to the other and then pulling the stitches tight.

Ears, arms, and legs are often sewn shut before they are attached. This is a running stitch. Attaching in this manner involves folding the raw edges in on a body piece. Here's how:

1 With upholstery thread and a needle, secure the thread at the seam as close to the folded edge as possible.

2 Sew around this edge, in and out with small stitches, returning to the seam again.

3 Pull stitches tight to gather the top of the body piece.

4 Secure the stitches and then the piece is attached to the body.

The gathers, especially in ears, add dimension to the body part. Animals do not have smooth limbs; they have joints and wrinkles and fur. By having gathered features, the animals have more personality.

Throughout the book, I use fabric glue to also attach body parts. It works very well with fabric, especially when adding elements, such as noses.

I often use it to attach parts that would be awkward to sew. It gives a strong bond. The slight odor disappears when the glue dries. When using the glue, it works best to apply the glue to the piece you are gluing. The glue is thick, so always apply it inside the edges of the piece so it does not press out beyond the nose or other body piece when you press it into place. I like the glue as an adhesive because it does not require heat to put it in place. With these toys being made from fleece, fur, or felt, pressing with an iron is not recommended.

Notice the gathers that appear where the dog ear is attached to the head. Such "wrinkles" make the animals more realistic.

Heads or Tails

Dudz Bear is just one of the toys whose head requires attachment with the method outlined in this section.

Many of the toys have heads that have to be sewn on. Again, upholstery thread is very strong and will secure the head really well. The area of the head to be sewn to the body should be a circular area, slightly smaller than the circumference of the bottom of the head. This prevents stitches from showing. Here's how it's done:

1 Place the head on the body to judge the area to be sewn.

2 Secure the thread at the top of the body within the area.

3 Take a small stitch through the head and back through body, moving in a small circle, as shown in the accompanying illustration. Do not pull the threads tight.

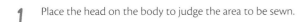

4 Once you have gone around the complete circle, pull the threads tight, bringing the head tight against the body.

5 Secure thread with several small stitches close together at back of body.

Tails can be pinned and sewn in the seam, but when some of the tails are really large like Catastrophe's, it is easier to leave an opening to insert the tail or sew it to the surface. The technique for sewing would be similar as for the head.

1 Secure the thread at base of the tail.

2 Sew around the tail, taking small stitches from the tail to the body back and forth.

3 Continue around the tail, pulling the stitches tight.

4 Secure the thread with several small stitches over the top of each other at base of body.

5 Clip the threads.

17

Friendly Faces

Use dimensional paint for a quick and easy way to create a face, like the one on Hairy-Etta shown here.

My favorite parts of these soft toys are their faces—big, happy, fun faces that just make you smile back. Eyes, eyelashes, noses, mouths, and whiskers all combine to make a face to delight any child.

With these soft toys, the face you are creating will be unique to you, the creator. A crooked smile or eye will just lend to the charm. I do find with faces that a slight alteration of a feature can change the total look of a face. Refer to the pattern pieces for placement of features but use your own judgment, too. With toys that are stuffed, the shape will vary slightly from person to person.

Below I explain several of the techniques that are used in the book to create all those charming faces.

One of the easiest faces to create is by using beads and dimensional paint. I really like Plaid's black shiny dimensional fabric paint. The paint has a thin nozzle that enables you to create a thin, consistent line for a smile like Hairy-Etta's and eyebrows or eyelashes. It is an easy way to create features, especially when the children are making them. Drawing the features first with a marker gives a good guideline to follow.

Eye beads or wiggly eyes can be glued in place to create a whole face in a matter of minutes. Of course, it must be set aside until the paint dries, but once it does, the paint is very durable.

For another option, use embroidery floss for the mouths or lashes. When using floss, cut a length about 18" to work with, then separate the strands. Usually, I like to work with two or three strands. To keep them from tangling, lay the strands side by side to put through the embroidery needle. Once the floss is secured, stitch the features by taking a stitch to one side of the mouth line and then to the opposite side. The pattern pieces are marked with the placement for all features. Use the disappearing marker for lighter faces.

The Eyes Have It

I believe the eyes are the most important aspect of any face you create. They bring a face to life.

There are black beads, wiggly eyes, teddy bear, and cat safety eyes all in different sizes to use for a toy. Black, white, and brown felt layered also make for good eyes on a large toy.

When sewing with black eye beads, I use them particularly for bears and other smaller animals. These eyes sink into the face, giving a very realistic appearance. The technique used is easy, as long as you use a sculpture needle to be able to reach through the head easily and upholstery thread for strength.

Several variations of eyes suitable for use on soft toys.

Felt, cut into the appropriate shapes, works wonderfully well for eyes, like that of Ted ZZZ Bear.

1 Secure the upholstery thread and sculpture needle at bottom of head.

2 Take the needle through the eye mark at the head front.

3 Slide on a bead over the needle.

4 Take the needle back through to the bottom of the head and pull the thread to indent bead in face.

5 Repeat steps 1 through 4 for the second eye bead.

6 Secure the thread at the bottom of the head.

When working with black eye beads, use a sculpture needle and upholstery thread. Secure the thread at the bottom of the head, as shown, continue through the eye mark, sliding the bead over the needle and then take the needle back through to the bottom of the head.

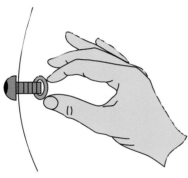

For toys that are going to be played with by younger children, use safety eyes. These are inserted before the animal is stuffed.

1 Make a small hole at each eye mark on face.

2 Insert the back of the eye through the hole.

3 Snap the safety ring into place. Be careful when snapping on the ring to push it completely on. Once they are part of the way on, the rings don't come back off and you will find yourself cutting another face or he could just wear an eye patch and become a pirate.

Snap the safety ring into place on the back of the safety eye piece.

Sniffin' and Snuffin'

Throughout the book there are many noses of many shapes. My favorite nose is just a felt nose, black or brown, glued on with fabric glue. Leather-look vinyl also makes a great dog nose. I do like my noses to be darker than the eyes or the same depth, but that's just a preference. Usually I have black noses, but if the material for the animal is colorful, then another color nose looks good like hot pink Wibbit Wabbit with her bright yellow nose.

Before gluing any nose permanently, just place it in position to make sure it looks the way you want it to. I like my noses close to the eyes, as I think it gives a more innocent look to the face.

My best advice is to have fun. When you look at the face you have created and you smile, then that is the perfect face!

Spots and Dots

When adding fabric polka-dots to fun fur, as shown here on Polkadilly Pooch, I recommend first pinning and then sewing them on, rather than gluing them, due to the difficulty in gluing on the nap of the fur.

I love polka-dots for their bright statements of color. I have always owned a polka-dotted dress; not that I look as cute as my toys wearing it, but I still love it. I used several fabrics in the book that have polka-dots in the design. After a few late nights, I started seeing dots on the fleece that weren't even there. I like to apply spots in just a couple of ways: either by attaching them with a small zigzag or buttonhole stitch or with fabric glue. With a material like fun fur, gluing is difficult because of the nap of the fur.

Pinning the spot or dot in place and sewing around it, taking the pins out as you go, works well with the fur. I use a tiny buttonhole stitch on my machine, going around the spot a couple of times.

Gluing spots and dots is fun, especially when deciding where they go after the animal is completed. Use a dimensional fabric paint to go around edges of spots for accent. This also keeps the spots from fraying. I like to do the painting around the spots before I glue them on, letting it dry thoroughly.

Pompons can be used to make fun spots and dots on smaller toys. They come in wonderful bright colors and give a fuzzy dimension to the toy. Fabric glue again secures them in place very quickly. It's an especially colorful way for kids to add more of their own personality to their toy. You will really be seeing dots for days!

Use a dimensional fabric paint around the edges of spots for accent and to keep the spots from fraying.

Pockets Full of Fun

Several of the toys have pockets for hiding treasures or books or pajamas. I think that for kids, and really for all of us, the element of surprise and discovery keeps life interesting. Kids love to think they can surprise you by hiding a favorite book or toy and then getting you to try to find it. Of course, if you have made the toy from the book, it's going to be really easy.

Most of the pockets in the book are constructed in the same manner. Because the animals are stuffed, the pocket pieces are in addition to the back of the toy, which is usually where the pocket is located. Here's how it's done:

1   Finish the pocket piece at its opening only.

2   Pin the wrong side of the pocket piece to the right side of the bottom or back piece of the toy. Pin very carefully when you have several layers so that you do not miss catching the pocket or back in the seam. Treat as just one piece of material.

3   Sew around the pocket edges so that when the animal is turned right-side out, the pocket is sewn in place.

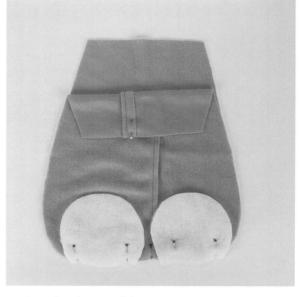

The pockets for most of the toys in this book are additions to the back of the toy. On Ted ZZZ Bear, shown here above unfinished and at left finished and all snuggled up to Charlie, both of the overlapping sides of the pocket were finished first. They were then overlapped, pinned, and treated as one back piece only, even though there were actually three pieces of fabric and three layers to sew through at the bottom and top.

All Together Now

Once all of the parts of the toy are ready to be put together, I have used several methods to attach them, some of which have already been described.

Method 1

One method that I really like enables the arms and legs to move. This is done by string jointing with a sculpture needle and upholstery thread or some people use dental floss. I prefer the thread.

Use at least a 4"-long needle so you do not lose it in the body and stab your fingers trying to find it. For jointing larger animals, there are needles 7" and longer (which are a little dangerous sometimes, especially if you gesture with your hands when you talk like I do).

To ensure the limbs move freely, there are two important details to remember. First, try to keep your stitches going back and forth through the body as close to the same spot as possible. Second, do not pull the thread so tight that the limbs are squeezed into the body. They should rest securely against the body. If they are too loose, they will dangle.

The Method 1 technique is as follows:

1 Secure the upholstery thread end at the arm placement on one side of the body with several small stitches.

2 Take the needle through the body piece, through one arm/leg, back through the arm/leg and the body, and then through and back through the other arm/leg, as shown.

3 Repeat step 2 three to four times.

4 Secure the thread under the arm and clip the threads.

Method 2

The other method for bringing everything together is just as important as the first. When you are creating some of the simpler toys with younger children, like Peewee Pup pictured here, try this technique:

1 Lay out all the pieces first, as shown, since kids tend to be very visual.

2 Tell the children what you are going to be doing first before starting. They can see the pictures in the book, as well as have everything they need in front of them.

3 Move on to the actual assembly of the toy, walking the children through each step.

I have just found it makes creating and sewing with kids much easier and everyone has fun. If they all have their pieces in front of them, it makes for creative harmony.

Wibbit Wabbit's arms, shown here draped lovingly around Megan, were attached with Method 1. The legs were attached that way, too!

21

chapter 2

PURRFECT PALS AND GRREAT BUDS

Pets and stuffed toys are perennial childhood favorites. Favorite pets for most children have been that special cat or dog that was dressed up, slept at the foot of the bed, or shared a drippy ice cream cone. Special memories abound with a cuddly childhood friend who is there to share the adventures of the day. Furry, friendly fun is captured in the cat and dog playmates in this chapter. Come play with Polkadilly Pooch, Catastrophe, Hot Dawg, Peewee Pup, and Skittles.

Hot Dawg

Sleepovers are an integral part of childhood. Staying up late, watching movies, and eating tons of popcorn with giggly friends is a favorite part of every kid's life. Hot Dawg is a friend from home to take on any sleepover adventure. With a body large enough to hold a cozy blanket or sleeping bag and pajamas, it is a great accessory for any child headed out the door on an overnight adventure. He also makes a great pillow. Here, Dylan and Hot Dawg are packed and ready for a weekend of fun, fun, fun. Remember Dylan: Hot Dawg is the No. 1 pillow fight champion. Have a great time.

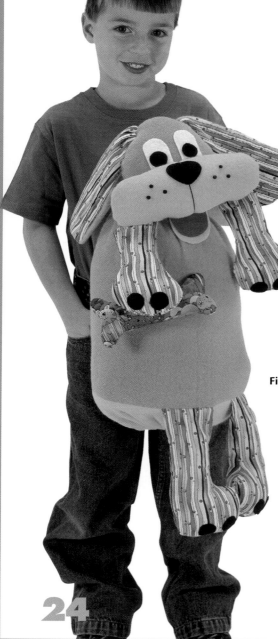

You Will Need

½-yard orange fleece
⅓-yard green fleece
½-yard striped fabric
⅛-yard print fabric
9" x 12" black felt
3" x 5" white felt
3" square red felt
8 oz. polyester fiberfill
½-yard black embroidery floss
6 black 5mm pompons
1 yard blue cording or heavy shoelace
1 yard 2"-wide plaid ribbon
⅓-yard ¼"-wide elastic
Fabric glue
Matching thread
Upholstery thread
Sewing machine
Upholstery needle
Needle
Scissors
Black fine marker
Disappearing marker
Pins
12 pattern pieces (#1)

Finished Size: 27" long and a big "hug" around

> **tip**
>
> Reviewing Chapter 1 before you begin will be very helpful in making the toys. The chapter is filled with detailed information about all aspects of completing the toys. Specific sections are clearly titled for easy reference. Also refer to the pattern pieces for specific placement details.

Cutting Plan

1 Hot Dawg is #1 on the pattern sheet. Using those pattern pieces and paying special attention to those that need to be cut as reverse pieces (R), cut as follows:
  - two head pieces from orange fleece
  - one 16" x 26" body piece from orange fleece
  - two muzzle pieces from green fleece
  - two ear pieces from green fleece
  - one mouth from green fleece
  - one 10½" x 26" bottom piece from green fleece
  - four front legs from striped fabric
  - four back legs from striped fabric
  - two ear pieces from striped fabric
  - two bones from print fabric
  - two outer eyes from white felt
  - two inner eyes from black felt
  - one nose from black felt
  - eight toes from black felt
  - one tongue from red felt

2 Cut the muzzle and head slits through one piece only of each where indicated on the pattern.

Making the Head

1 Place right sides together for the legs, ears, muzzle, and head, and sew together with a ¼" seam allowance, being sure to leave a turn hole.

2 Trim all curves.

3 Turn each piece right-side out.

4 Glue black toe circles to the front feet.

5 Stuff the front legs, leaving 2" from the top empty. Turn tops under on the front legs.

6 Pin the front legs to the back of the muzzle on either side of the slit and with upholstery thread and needle, sew legs in place, as shown, with a small running stitch. Repeat second row of stitching over the first.

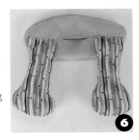

7 Stuff the muzzle and latch the slit opening closed with a ladder stitch.

8 Tie black floss around the center of the muzzle, knotting at the muzzle back.

9 Turn the tops of the ears under and sew a small running stitch through the top of each ear. Pull the stitches tight. Leave threads attached.

10 Pin the ears on the head and sew in place with several stitches, as shown.

11 Stuff the head and sew the slit opening shut.

12 Glue the muzzle to the head.

13 Referring to the accompanying photo for placement, glue the black felt eye pieces to the white felt eyes and then glue the finished eyes to face. Glue the nose and pompons in place on muzzle. Glue the tongue to the mouth piece and then glue the straight end of the finished mouth in place.

14 Set the head aside to dry thoroughly.

Making the Body

1 Press ½" hem on one long side of the orange strip. This will be the top of the body. Machine-stitch close to the inside edge.

2 Press ¼" under on one long side of the green strip and then press under again 1¼" to create casing for the bottom. Sew close to the inside edge, leaving room to thread the cord through.

3 Stuff the back legs, leaving top 2" empty.

4 Center and pin the leg ends to the opposite edge of orange strip right-side up.

5 Place the right side of the green strip on top of orange right-side down, pin, and sew the pieces together with ¼" seam, as shown in photo 5A. Sew again along seam line for the completed look of free-hanging legs, as shown in 5B.

6 Lay the stitched piece flat and then fold it in half, right sides together, matching the raw edges. Sew from one stitch line to the opposite stitch line with ¼" seam. Repeat. This forms the tube body.

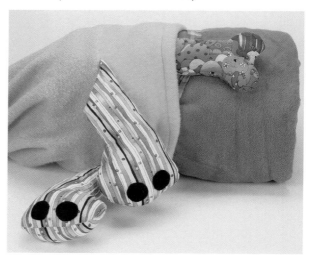

The blanket inserted into the tube body.

7 String elastic through the top of the body, pulling as tight as possible. Sew or tie ends of elastic together, trimming off extra and tucking the ends into the casing.

8 String the cord through the bottom casing. Knot several times at the ends to keep them from sliding through the casing.

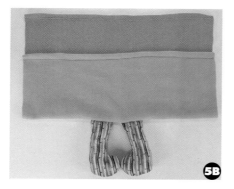

Finishing the Toy

1 With the upholstery thread doubled, attach the head to the top of the body. Stitch around in a circle, following the outside edge of the upper closing, as shown.

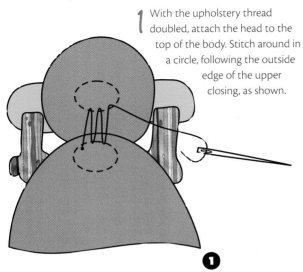

2 Cut slits in one side of a bone piece and then sew the bone pieces, right sides together.

3 Turn through the slits, stuff the bone, and sew the slit openings shut.

4 Glue the bone to the back of the right paw, with the sewn opening glued to the paw, as shown.

5 Glue the second bone to the ribbon, roll up the blanket, and tie the ribbon around, as shown.

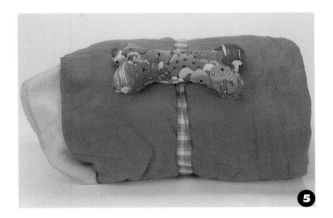

There's no way anyone could get homesick on an overnight sleepover with a happy friend like Hot Dawg to keep him company.

tip *Two fleece blankets 50" x 60" fit inside Hot Dawg. Sew three sides of the blankets together to create a cozy sleeping pouch. Pajamas can be rolled up in the middle.*

PeeWee Pup

Small but mighty, PeeWee Pup is a tag-along friend to fasten to a backpack or jacket. Those first days of school can be a little scary away from home, so PeeWee can be a piece of home always on hand for a quick pat or cuddle. Kids and parents can make this quick and easy little fella together. Make a bunch in different colors for birthday gifts. From the big grin on Jared's face here, he and PeeWee are ready for their day together at school.

You Will Need

5" x 26" blue fleece
9" x 12" felt pieces, one each in the following colors:
- red
- antique white
- black

2 black 6mm beads
Fuzzy green hair elastic
Zipper clip
2 red ½" pompons
6 oz. polyester fiberfill
Black dimensional fabric paint (optional)
Fabric glue
Upholstery thread
Needle
Scissors
Black fine marker
7 pattern pieces (#2)

Finished Size: 6" long

Cutting Plan

1 PeeWee is #2 on the pattern sheet. Using those pattern pieces, cut as follows:
   - one body piece from blue fleece
   - one head piece from blue fleece
   - one body bottom from blue fleece.
   - two ears from red felt
   - two tail pieces from red felt
   - one body bottom piece from red felt
   - two bone pieces from antique white felt
   - one nose from black felt
     (or use red pompon for a brighter nose)

tip

Reviewing Chapter 1 before you begin will be very helpful in making the toys. The chapter is filled with detailed information about all aspects of completing the toys. Specific sections are clearly titled for easy reference. Also refer to the pattern pieces for specific placement details.

Putting It Together

1 Glue blue and red body bottom pieces together. Glue the tail pieces together.

2 Sew a small running stitch around the body and head circles, as shown below left. Pull stitches to create a cup shape and insert a small ball of stuffing. Pull stitches tighter, as shown, and secure threads on the body and head, leaving the needle attached to bottom of head.

3 Squeeze the head into an oval shape and take a needle from the bottom through to the top of the oval. Insert one bead on the needle and take the needle back through the head to the bottom of the head. Pull thread to indent eye into fleece. Repeat for second eye, as shown below. Secure threads at the bottom of the head.

4 Squeeze the body into an oval shape and then lay the body and head flat on table. Push them together and glue.

5 Referring to the photo for placement, put a small dot of glue at the top of each ear and glue them to either side of the head. Glue pompons together at the end of the head for the muzzle. Glue nose in place at center of pompons with a small dot of glue.

9 Turn the body over, as shown, and squeeze glue in the center of the body bottom and the bone. Glue both pieces in place.

6 Squeeze a small amount of glue on the tail base. Center the tail on the body back, placing it in an upright position, and glue the tail in place. Hold for a few seconds.

7 Place elastic over the neck for a collar.

8 Sew clasp to center of one bone, as shown below.

10 Optional: Referring to the accompanying photos, squeeze black paint to dot the muzzle with three spots on either side of nose. Draw two tiny foot lines with paint on each paw.

When sewing with kids to make PeeWee, have the needles double-threaded with a knot at the end. Kids can get frustrated when they are sewing and the needle comes off the thread. For younger children, cut the pieces out for them and omit the paint. Wiggly eyes could also be used in place of beads and just glued on. Creating a fun and frustration-free creative experience is the goal for both children and parents. Making a mess though is totally acceptable. There is nothing like scraps and bits of bright color all around to spark the imagination.

tip

Catastrophe

Just hanging around and being totally silly is a great way to spend time when you're a kid. Having a silly yellow-and-purple cat to hang around and be super-silly with is even better. Catastrophe is just the right cat for the job. Little magnets in his colorful spots make him able to touch his nose, toes, and ears, or allow him to twist into a purple pretzel. Hanging out on a lazy day with a favorite kid is Catastrophe's favorite place to be.

You Will Need

½-yard yellow fleece
½-yard purple or fuchsia brushed fleece
15 bright 3" fabric scrap squares
3" square white felt scrap
Black dimensional fabric paint
10 ceramic magnets (Darice)
2 15mm safety cat eyes (Bel*Tree)
Fabric glue
Masking tape
Iron and board
Matching thread
Upholstery thread
Sewing machine
Needle
Scissors
Black fine marker
Disappearing marker
Pins
6 pattern pieces (#3)

Finished Size: 16"

Cutting Plan

1 Catastrophe is #3 on the pattern sheet. Using those pattern pieces and paying special attention to those that need to be cut as reverse pieces (R), cut as follows:
   - two head pieces from yellow fleece
   - one upper body piece from yellow fleece
   - one lower body piece from yellow fleece
   - two tail pieces from purple fleece
   - one reverse upper body piece from purple fleece
   - one reverse lower body piece from purple fleece
   - one nose lining from white felt
   - one nose piece from a print scrap
   - 14 spots from the print scraps (Note the special instructions in Add the Spots steps 1 through 3 before cutting.)

2 Cut the slit, as indicated on the pattern, for one of the head pieces.

Making the Body

1 Place right sides of one top and one bottom body piece together. With ¼" seam allowance, sew the center seams, leaving an opening in bottom. Repeat for the other top and bottom pieces.

2 Line up both of the stitched body pieces, right sides together. With a ¼" seam allowance, sew around and repeat again to reinforce, leaving an opening for the tail. Clip curves. Turn right-side out.

3 Place the tail pieces right sides together. With a ¼" seam allowance, sew seam around tail. Repeat for extra durability. Turn right-side out.

4 Stuff the body with small pieces of fiberfill. Start at the end of each foot, filling towards the center of the body.

5 Secure the upholstery thread and needle at one end of the body opening. Sew the body opening shut with small stitches from side-to-side, as shown, and pull the stitches tight. Secure thread at opposite end with several tiny stitches on top of each other.

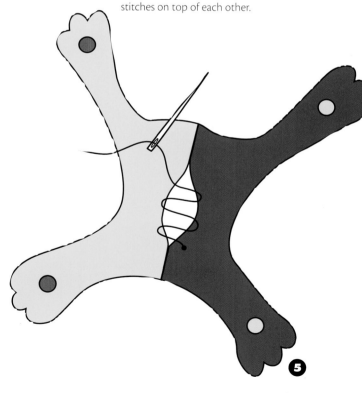

5

6 Stuff the tail with small pieces of fiberfill, beginning at the tip. Smooth and shape with your hands as you go. The tail will curve some as it is stuffed. Sew end of tail shut.

7 Insert tail into opening at end of body. With the needle and upholstery thread, sew the tail in place with small stitches around the tail, as shown. Alternate stitches from tail to body as you stitch around the tail. Secure the thread with tiny stitches on the underside of the tail.

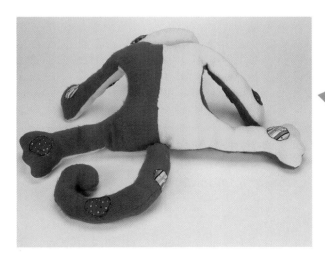

Finished head.

Making the Head

1 Assemble all the materials needed for the head: fleece pieces, eyes, dimensional fabric paint, nose pieces, sharp scissors, and masking tape.

2 Place the fabric nose piece wrong-side up and then lay the felt nose lining in the center of the fabric nose.

3 Press fabric nose edges over felt lining around entire nose.

4 Use fabric glue to glue the fabric edges of the nose in place.

Catastrophe's underside with the tail attached.

tip

Finish all face features before inserting the safety eyes. The backs of the safety eyes would keep the piece from lying flat, making it difficult to work on.

5 Place the front head piece right-side up on the work surface and use a piece of tape on each side to hold head in place.

6 Referring to the photo of the finished head, use the marker to mark the placement of the eyes and then outline the whiskers, dots, mouth, and eyebrows. Glue nose in place.

7 Follow all marked lines with fabric paint. Let the paint dry.

8 With the sharp points of scissors, make tiny holes for eyes. Insert the safety eyes and snap on the backs securely.

9 Place the head pieces right sides together. With ¼" seam allowance, sew completely around seam. Repeat to reinforce. Turn right-side out through slit. Stuff beginning with ear tips first.

10 Sew the slit in the back of the head shut the same, as shown in step 5 illustration for body. Set aside the head.

tip

Magnets need to be the super-strong button type to attract each other through the fabric. Make sure when putting the magnets in place that the positive side is out. Not every spot needs a magnet. It is important to have one in each foot, the head, chin, ear, and tail.

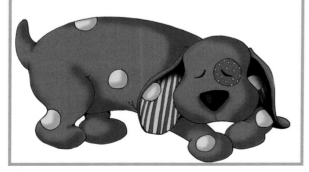

Adding the Spots

1 Draw spots on right side of fabric scraps with black marker.

2 Follow along the black line on the spots with the black fabric paint. Let dry.

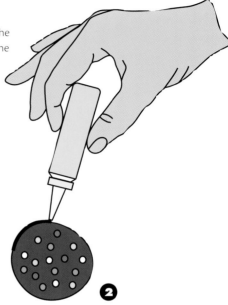

❷

3 Cut spots out carefully with sharp scissors. Set aside.

4 Mark the placement of the spots on the legs, head, and body. Refer to photo and the pattern head piece for spot placements, if necessary. With a small dab of glue in the center of each spot, glue each magnet in place, as shown.

❹

5 With upholstery thread and needle, sew the magnets to the body, tail, and head pieces. First knot the thread and secure it at one side of magnet. Then take the thread across the magnet to the opposite side, go through the fleece under the magnet to come out at opposite side, and repeat to crisscross magnet, as shown.

6 Use fabric glue around the wrong side edge of each fabric spot piece. Glue the fabric pieces in place over the secured magnets.

Finishing the Toy

1 Secure the thread on the body, as marked on pattern piece.

2 Alternating between the head and body, sew around in a small circle, approximately 1" in diameter, as shown in the accompanying illustration. Pull the stitches tight and secure the thread with several small stitches at underside of head.

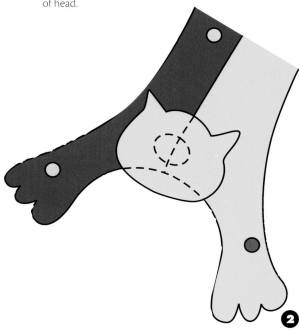

Polkadilly Pooch

A dog, whether it's brown or black or even bright red with yellow polka-dots, is a boy's best friend. Polkadilly is a cuddly, furry friend with a secret pocket to hold a favorite bedtime story and a flashlight! He can sit and shake his head "yes" while listening to stories shared between friends. His sleepy eyes can calm the most active kid, and together, they will drift off to a dreamland filled with fun.

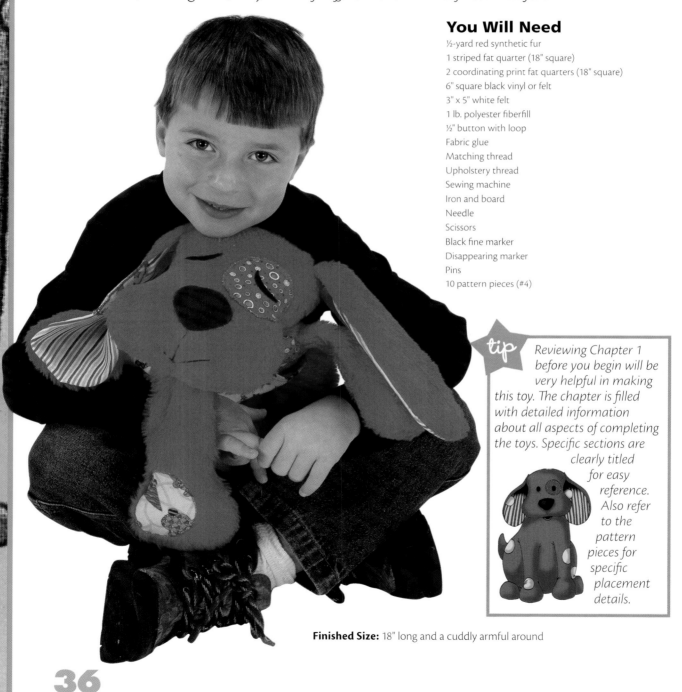

You Will Need

½-yard red synthetic fur
1 striped fat quarter (18" square)
2 coordinating print fat quarters (18" square)
6" square black vinyl or felt
3" x 5" white felt
1 lb. polyester fiberfill
½" button with loop
Fabric glue
Matching thread
Upholstery thread
Sewing machine
Iron and board
Needle
Scissors
Black fine marker
Disappearing marker
Pins
10 pattern pieces (#4)

> **tip**
>
> *Reviewing Chapter 1 before you begin will be very helpful in making this toy. The chapter is filled with detailed information about all aspects of completing the toys. Specific sections are clearly titled for easy reference. Also refer to the pattern pieces for specific placement details.*

Finished Size: 18" long and a cuddly armful around

Lay the fur with the nap down. Lay the pattern pieces in the same direction on the fur. This will give the dog a natural feel when he is patted. Draw pattern pieces on wrong side of fur. Cut with sharp scissors just through the fur backing not the fibers. When sewing the seams, tuck the fur in along the edges. If any fur gets caught in seam, pull it out with a needle. Brush the seams.

Cutting Plan

1. Polkadilly is #4 on the pattern sheet. (Be sure to include the two leg pieces, the nose, and the ear that are marked for both Polkadilly and Hot Dawg.) Using those pattern pieces and paying special attention to those that need to be cut as reverse pieces (R), cut as follows:
   - two head pieces from red fur
   - two upper body pieces from red fur
   - four back leg pieces from red fur
   - four front leg pieces from red fur
   - two ear pieces (outer ear) from red fur
   - one tail piece (outer tail) from red fur
   - two ear pieces (inner ear) from striped fabric
   - one bottom body piece from print fabric
   - one pocket piece from print fabric
   - one tail piece (inner tail) from print fabric
   - 12 spot pieces from print fabrics
   - one nose piece from vinyl/felt
   - two eye pieces from vinyl/felt

Preparing the Pieces

1. Pin the spots to the legs and body, as shown at right, with one or two on each leg, alternating them, and three on the upper body pieces. Pin one to the face, referring to the pattern piece for placement. Set ear dots aside.

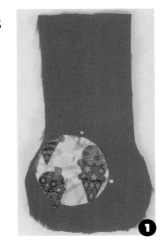

2. With red thread, use a small buttonhole stitch to sew around each spot, as shown. Repeat for a heavier outline on dots, if desired. Clip all threads.

3. Place right sides together and sew the legs, ears, and head pieces together, ¼" seam allowance. Trim all curves and turn each piece right-side out.

Making the Head

1. Center and pin one spot on either ear so that half of the dot is on either side of the ear. Pin one spot to the front of the right ear and the other spot to the back of the left ear.

2. Buttonhole stitch around the half-dot on the outer ear, sewing through all layers. Repeat for the other ear. Clip the threads.

3. Referring to the head pattern piece, make a small hole in the head back only.

4. Stuff the head, but do not sew the opening shut yet.

5. Referring to the accompanying photo, glue the nose and eyes in place.

6. Press in ½" at the top of each ear. With upholstery thread and needle sew across top of each ear with a small running stitch. Pull the stitches tight.

7 Place the ears in position on the head, as shown, and sew in place with several small stitches.

8 Insert the button in the head back with the loop out. Place the needle through the loop to keep the button in place. With upholstery thread and needle, handstitch around the button with tiny stitches, as shown.

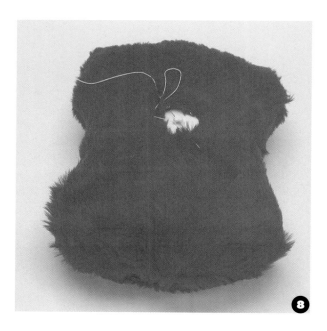

9 Pull stitches tight and secure the thread with a couple more tiny stitches and then sew the head opening shut in the seam with a ladder stitch. Leave the needle and thread attached. Set the head aside.

Making the Body

1 Sew the upper body pieces with right sides together, leaving a tail opening.

2 Press the pocket piece on the fold, wrong sides together.

3 Place the pocket piece on top of the bottom piece, right sides together. Then place the upper body on top, right sides together and pin in place. Tuck the fur in along the edges. Pin on either side of each opening.

4 Sew the layered pieces with ¼" seam allowance, noting the unsewn areas for leg insertion. Repeat the stitching again for durability. Trim the threads and turn right-side out.

5 Stuff the legs, leaving 1" from the top empty.

6 Insert legs into each opening on the body and pin in place, referring to accompanying photo for placement.

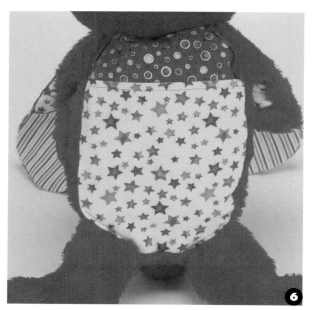

7 Pleat the tail by bringing both lines together, as marked on pattern piece. Finger-press flat. Sew a couple stitches at the bottom of the tail to hold the pleat.

8 Insert the tail into the body opening, with the inner tail facing out.

9 With upholstery thread and needle, sew the legs and tail in place, as shown below. Sew back and forth through the body and leg with small stitches. Secure the threads with small stitches sewn together.

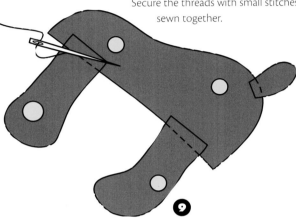

Attaching the Head

1 Attach the head by taking the needle through the loop to the body, as shown. (Refer to pattern piece for exact placement.)

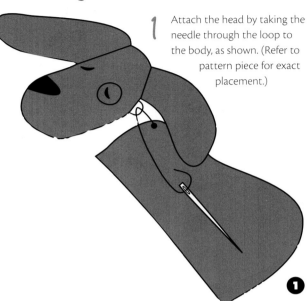

10 Stuff the body softly. Turn the raw edges of the body opening under ½" and sew around opening with upholstery thread and needle, making small stitches. Pull stitches tight to close the opening. Take several stitches to hold. Clip threads.

2 Sew back and forth between the body and through the button loop several times. Sew small stitches on top of each other at the body to secure threads. Clip the threads. The head will move back and forth when sewn in this fashion.

tip

Make a bone from the Hot Dawg pattern for Polkadilly Pooch, too. Every dog needs a bone to play with. Cut two bones pieces from felt and glue them together. Polkadilly can play with the bone, and it can also be tucked in the pocket as a bookmark.

Skittles the Kitten

Kids have lots of stuff—small, fun stuff. Because they are always going here and there, that small stuff sometimes gets lost in transition. Skittles comes to the rescue. The tail is a great handle for this chubby, soft bag and the back opening can hold all kinds of things. Inside, a couple of fishy friends have been swallowed up, but fish them out easily, and they become bags to hold even more accessories or little toys. The large button closure is also a great hook for the fish to hang from. Skittles, so soft and cozy, can be a handy tote, comfy pillow for a tired little head, or just a huggable friend.

You Will Need

½-yard teal furry polar fleece
⅛-yard orange sherpa
⅓-yard cotton polyester print fabric
9" x 12" felt pieces, one of each in the following colors:

- yellow
- green
- peacock
- orange
- white
- red
- black

1 lb. polyester fiberfill
Black dimensional fabric paint
1" bright button
8 bright fuzzy hair elastics
2 stretchy nylon hair bands
2 white ¼" pompons
Fabric glue
Matching thread
Upholstery thread
Sewing machine
Iron and board
Needle
Scissors
Black fine marker
Disappearing marker
Pins
13 pattern pieces (#5)

Finished Size: 21", from the tip of her tail to her bright orange paws

Cutting Plan

1   Skittles is #5 on the pattern sheet. Using those pattern pieces and paying special attention to those that need to be cut as reverse pieces (R), cut as follows:

- one pocket piece (outer pocket) from teal fleece
- two head pieces from teal fleece
- eight paw pieces from orange sherpa
- one pocket piece from print fabric
- two outer muzzle pieces from print fabric
- two tail pieces from print fabric
- one nose piece from black felt
- two inner eye pieces from black felt
- one tongue piece from red felt
- two inner muzzle pieces from white felt
- two "Fish A" pieces from orange felt
- two "Fish B" pieces from yellow felt
- two "Fish A" fins from peacock felt
- two "Fish A" slit opening reinforcement strips from peacock felt
- two outer eye pieces from green felt
- two "Fish B" fins from green felt
- two "Fish B" slit opening reinforcement strips from green felt

2   Cut a slit in one head piece, as indicated on the pattern piece. This is the head front.

3   Cut slits in four paw pieces, as indicated on the pattern.

4   Cut slits in each of the "Fish A" and "Fish B" pieces, as instructed on the pattern. These are the fish fronts.

tip

Reviewing Chapter 1 before you begin will be very helpful in making the toys. The chapter is filled with detailed information about all aspects of completing the toys. Specific sections are clearly titled for easy reference. Also refer to the pattern pieces for specific placement details.

Making the Pocket

1   Pin the orange hair elastic (button loop) to the center of the pocket straight edge, as marked on pattern piece.

2   With right sides together, as shown in photo 2A, sew the top straight side of the back pocket pieces together for the finished look shown in photo 2B.

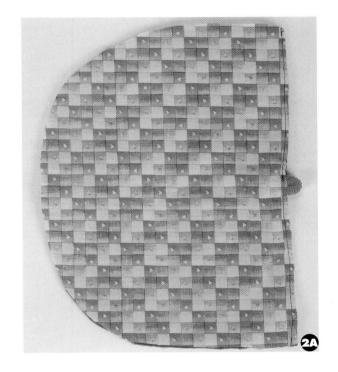

2A

2B

3 Turn right-side out and press gently along the seam on the inner pocket fabric side.

4 Match the inner fabric pocket to the right side of the fleece back head piece, as shown below, and then place the right side of the front head piece on top. Pin and sew all three pieces together, repeating the stitching a second time for extra durability. Clip the threads and curves and turn this head-pocket piece right-side out through the front slit opening.

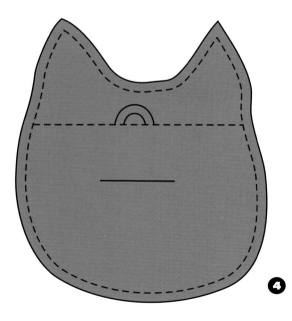

5 Stuff the head, beginning with the ears.

6 With upholstery thread and a needle, sew the front opening shut with small, back-and-forth stitches. Secure the thread with several small stitches and clip the thread ends.

7 Smooth pocket flat, centering the loop.

8 Sew the button onto the back head piece to fasten loop over, as shown.

Making the Face

1 Center each white felt muzzle circle on the wrong side of each fabric muzzle circle, as shown below.

2 Glue around the felt muzzle pieces, turning the fabric outer muzzle edges over the felt, as shown. Press in place with your fingers, working around each circle.

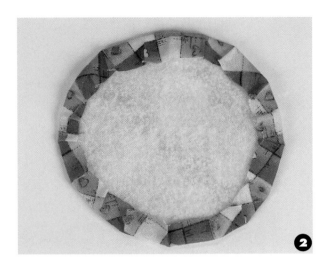

3 With disappearing marker and using the pattern piece as a guide, draw the whiskers on each muzzle piece. Then draw over this line with fabric paint, as shown, and set aside to dry.

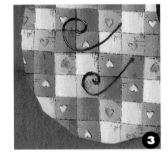

4 Layer the black felt eye pieces on the green felt eye pieces, glue together, and then glue the white pompons on, as shown.

5 Place the tongue on the front of the head and then place the muzzle pieces side-by-side over the top of the tongue. Position the nose and eyes on the face.

6 Lift each face piece, beginning with the eyes, and glue them in place, for a finished look as shown. Let dry.

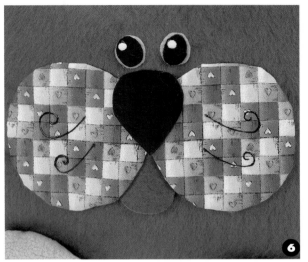

Finishing this Cat

1 Use fabric paint to draw paw lines on the front two feet. Let dry.

2 With right sides together on each of the four sets of paw pieces, sew the paws.

3 Turn the paws through the slits, stuff, and sew the openings shut with upholstery thread and needle. Secure and clip the threads.

4 Referring to the pattern piece and the step 8 photo, if necessary, glue the feet in place. Let dry. Skittles should stand.

5 Sew the tail pieces, right sides together.

6 Clip the curves, turn right-side out, and stuff the tail firmly with small pieces of fiberfill, beginning at the curved end of the tail.

7 Turn the open end of tail in ½" and use upholstery thread and needle to sew around the end, pulling the stitches tight.

43

8 Sew the tail in place at the top of the head, as marked on pattern piece and in accompanying photo, with small stitches around tail twice. Secure the threads with several small stitches close together.

9 Line up the hair elastics and use upholstery thread to sew through the loops. Then, sew them to the top of the head in front of the tail, as shown. Secure threads.

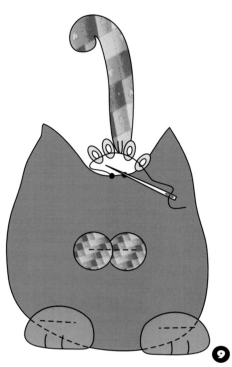

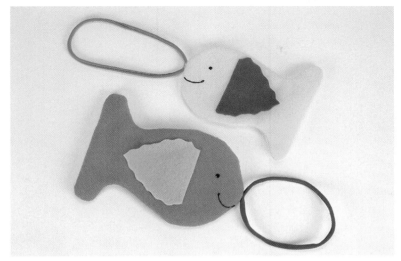

The finished fish can come in an array of different colors, depending on the likes of your child. Just adjust the felt colors in the materials list to match what you'd like to use.

Making the Fish

1   With right sides together, sew each fish and carefully turn.

2   Slit and glue the felt reinforcement pieces to openings on both Fish A and Fish B.

3   Glue the fins in place on each fish, as shown, so that they cover the reinforcement pieces.

4   With disappearing pen, mark the eyes and mouth on each fish, referring to pattern pieces and photo at right for placement, as necessary. Then, draw over these lines with fabric paint. Do one side, then the other, letting each side dry before turning.

5   Sew the loops in place on each fish and hang them from the button at the back of the kit bag or put them inside the bag's pocket.

tip

Kids can sew, with contrasting thread or floss, around the fish to create their own colorful "school" to share or use as gifts. For younger ones, make sure to thread and knot the needle for them. Fill these fish with candy, stickers, lip gloss, or hair stuff. Or hang fish from a brightly painted dowel for a party centerpiece and pass them out as favors at the end.

3

4

chapter 3

WIGGLES, JIGGLES, AND LOTS OF GIGGLES

Kids hardly ever sit still. Playing, exploring, and being active are part of the joys of being a child. Toys and games that encourage active play are always popular. The toys in this chapter are still soft to the touch, but even better, they are also games. They can be played with a friend or just enjoyed alone. Simply silly, these toys are sure to create "lots of giggles" for sure. Say hello to Wacky Wilma, Oh Ladybug, Fred Frog, Tuttles Turtle, and Butterfly Flower.

Wacky Wilma

Playing games is always fun for children. Kids have enjoyed even the simplest of games, like ring-toss, for many years. This game of ring-toss is a little girl's delight with a silly goose to play with. Soft, feathery rings can be thrown over Wilma's head or on her chubby feet. Cute little Vanessa loved playing with Wilma. Feathers and giggles filled the air.

You Will Need

¼-yard hot pink fleece
½-yard lime green fleece
⅛-yard yellow velour
¼-yard quilt batt
3 cotton print fat quarters
1 lb. polyester fiberfill
2 white 2" pompons
2 black 12mm beads
2 white feather boas
12" foam pipe wrap
12" x 18" piece white Flexi-Foam
Fabric glue
42" length 26-gauge wire
Matching thread
Upholstery thread
Sewing machine
Iron and board
Needle
Scissors
Fiskars Soft Grip Wave Scissors
Black fine marker
Disappearing marker
Pins
10 pattern pieces (#6)

Finished Size: 30" from her hot pink head to her not-so-dainty feet!

48

Cutting Plan

1. Wacky Wilma is #6 on the pattern sheet. Using those pattern pieces and paying special attention to those that need to be cut as reverse pieces (R), cut as follows:
   - two body pieces from pink fleece
   - one body bottom from pink fleece
   - two head pieces from pink fleece
   - two neck pieces from green fleece
   - four leg pieces from green fleece
   - two beak pieces from yellow velour
   - four feet from yellow velour
   - two feather pieces from the first cotton print
   - four feather pieces from the second cotton print
   - four feather pieces from the third cotton print
   - 10 feather pieces from quilt batt
   - 9" x 12" piece from quilt batt
   - two inner lining wing pieces from foam

2. Using wave scissors and the appropriate patterns, cut as follows:
   - four main wing pieces from green fleece
   - two outer wings from the first cotton print

Making the Head and Body

1. Work with one side of head/body at a time, sewing all pieces right sides together. Begin by sewing one beak piece to the corresponding head piece, matching small dots.

2. Sew one neck piece to the corresponding head-beak piece, matching large dots.

3. Sew one neck-head-beak piece to the corresponding body piece, matching the squares.

4. Repeat steps 1 through 3 for the other side of Wilma's head/body.

5. Pin both head/body pieces right sides together, carefully matching where each piece joins. (The neck opening is at the back.) Sew ¼" seam from the top of the head down on one side to the end of the body. Repeat for the other side. Clip all curves and threads.

6. Pin the body bottom to the body, matching the front (F) and back (B), as marked by triangles on pattern pieces. Sew ¼" seam. Clip curves.

7. Stuff the beak and head firmly with fiberfill.

8. Lay pipe wrap on the 9" x 12" quilt batt piece, as shown, and roll it up. The quilt batt should wrap around twice. Use fabric glue to hold the quilt batt in place.

8

tip To make sure the body and neck are stuffed as firmly as possible, let the body with openings set overnight. The fiberfill will settle slightly. Fill with more fiberfill in the morning. If the body gets distorted slightly as the fleece stretches, firmly mold it into shape with your hands.

9   Insert pipe wrap piece into the neck, as shown. It will extend into the body slightly. Center the pipe wrap piece inside the neck. If there is any remaining space in the neck, fill it with more fiberfill.

10   Pin the neck opening closed while the rest of the body is stuffed. Finish stuffing the body firmly.

11   With matching thread and a latch stitch, sew the openings shut on the body bottom and the neck.

9

Adding the Beak and Legs

1   Secure upholstery thread and needle on the seam line where the beak meets the head. Take the needle through the center of a pompon, through an eye bead, and back through the pompon to the seam line. Repeat the stitch to secure, pulling the thread tight at the end.

2   Repeat step 1 for the other eye, this time securing the thread with small stitches under pompon at the end.

3   Squirt a little fabric glue under the edges of the pompons for extra strength.

4   Sew the feet to the leg pieces, right sides together.

5   Match the feet-leg pieces and sew together with ¼" seam allowance, leaving the top of the legs open.

6   Stuff the feet and then the legs with fiberfill, leaving 1" empty at the top of each leg.

7   Turn the tops of the legs in ½" and use upholstery thread to sew across the tops of the legs by machine or hand.

7

8   Pin the legs in place on the body, referring to the accompanying photo for help with positioning, if necessary. Flip Wilma so the back of its legs are in a good position for sewing. Secure the upholstery thread and needle at one end of a leg and sew tiny stitches back and forth between the leg and the body, all around the leg returning to the back. Secure the thread.

9   Repeat step 8 for the second leg.

10   Measure around the leg, just above the foot and then cut two pieces of feather boa, adding 1" to the measurement for each.

11   Place the boa pieces around the bottom of each foot, as shown above, and glue the ends together, pressing into glue.

11

Feather pieces can be mixed in any combination for Wilma and same-print pieces do not have to be matched up. Remember that when sewing with quilt batt, it may catch in the machine. To help, place a layer of waxed paper underneath the quilt batt and sew. Just tear the waxed paper away afterwards.

8 Stitch through the feathers to the body several times, catching all feathers. Secure the thread at back of tail feathers for a finished look like that in the accompanying photo.

Adding the Tail Feathers

1 Layer the feathers right sides together, with two layers of quilt batt on the bottom.

2 Sew around each of the five feathers.

3 Turn each wing right-side out and then turn the bottom end in ½" on each. Press.

4 With upholstery thread and needle, secure thread at edge of one wing and sew small stitches through the wing, pulling tight to gather the bottom. Without cutting the thread, take the needle through the second wing bottom. Pull the stitches tight as before and secure thread at the end. Cut threads.

5 Repeat step 4 for two more feathers.

6 Stitch remaining feather only with the upholstery thread, as in step 4, but not attaching it to any other feathers.

7 Layer the feathers on top of each other with the single feather on the bottom and then sew in place on the body, as shown, with upholstery thread and needle.

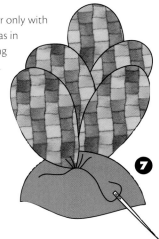

Adding the Wings

1 Glue the outer wing pieces to the centers of the two main wings, as shown.

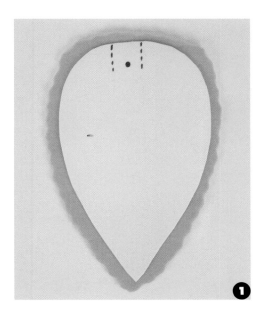

2 Mark the pleat on the foam for the wings and then place the foam in between the wrong sides of the outer wings, as shown.

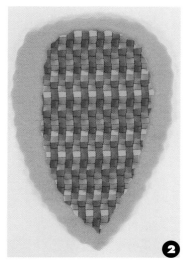

3 Topstitch ¼" around the outer wings with either matching or contrasting thread—your choice.

4 Make a pleat in each wing by matching the dotted lines and sew along these lines. Finger-press the center of the pleat flat.

5 Secure upholstery thread and needle at wing position on one side of body, and referring to the accompanying photo for guidance, place each wing in position on either side of the body.

6 Sew through each wing back, through the body, and out the opposite side of the body through the other wing. Repeat this thread path, pulling the thread snugly to the body. (Refer to Chapter 1, page 21, for more assistance with this method of sewing, if necessary.) Secure the thread under one wing on the body. Clip threads.

Making the Feather Rings

1 Cut three 16" pieces of wire and three boa pieces the same length.

2 Bend the ends of wire into small loops, as shown, and then twist the wire and boa together.

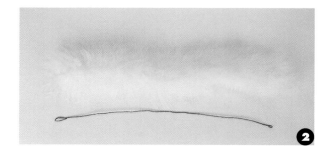

3 Hook the loops of wire into each other. Squeeze closed.

4 Glue the ends of the boa together at the wire loops, making sure no rough edge of wire can be felt.

5 Repeat steps 2 through 4 for the other two wire and boa pieces.

Oh Ladybug

Ladybug, ladybug, fly away home. How many times have we heard that familiar childhood refrain? This lucky ladybug carries her babies with her in a handy pocket. Even better, when the babies come out to play, they become a fun game of dominoes. Match the dots on their wings side-by-side. Here, Megan and Dylan are all set to play!

You Will Need

¼-yard red felt
⅓-yard black felt
6 oz. polyester fiberfill
4 mm black pompons
2 wiggly eyes
1 skein red embroidery floss
Fabric glue
Matching thread
Sewing machine
Needle
Scissors
Fiskars Soft-Grip scallop scissors
Black fine marker
White chalk
Pins
5 pattern pieces (#7)

Finished Size: 11"

Cutting Plan

1 Ladybug is #7 on the pattern sheet. Using those pattern pieces and paying special attention to those that need to be cut as reverse pieces (R), cut as follows:

- two body pieces from black felt
- 16 baby body pieces from black felt
- 10 spots from black felt
- one pocket piece from red felt
- two outer wing pieces from red felt
- two inner wing pieces from red felt
- 16 baby wing pieces from red felt

2 Cut a slit in one body piece, as indicated on the pattern piece.

Making the Ladybug

1 Using the pattern as a guide, draw a mouth on the head with chalk.

2 With two strands of the red floss, secure the floss at the back of the mouth line, bringing the needle through the center of the mouth. Make one long stitch to the end of mouth line, take the needle through to the back, go through the center once again, and make a long stitch to the opposite mouth line. Take the needle to the back again and secure the thread.

3 Glue on the eyes above the stitched mouth.

4 Pin body pieces together with the slit piece on top and the pocket piece on the bottom and topstitch completely around, as shown below.

5 Stuff the body with fiberfill.

6 With needle and thread, stitch the slit shut, as shown at right, and secure the thread at both ends.

7 Glue the outer and inner wings together, glue the spots on the wings (five on each wing), and then glue the wings to the top of the ladybug body, as shown at right.

Finished ladybug.

Making the Baby Bugs

1. With black marker, draw a line to mark the center of the wings on the babies, as shown at right.

2. Glue the pompons on the wings, varying the number of pompons on each from one to six.

3. Glue the spotted wings on top of baby bodies, as shown.

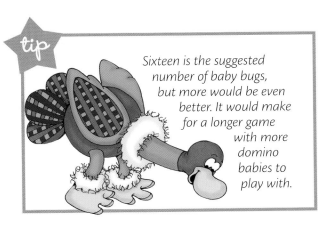

How to Play: *For two players, place all the babies in the pocket. Each player pulls out five babies apiece. The first player with the baby having the least number of spots places it on the Lady's back. The next player matches a baby with the same number of spots to the first one. The play continues until someone has played all his or her babies. If someone can't play at his or her turn, he or she must pick another baby out of the pocket.*

Sixteen is the suggested number of baby bugs, but more would be even better. It would make for a longer game with more domino babies to play with.

Megan shows that this game is just as fun when played with one!

Fred Frog

Fred Frog is such a happy guy with that great big grin. He loves his bugs; the brightly colored bean bag bugs fly through the air to be swallowed up in that gaping mouth. Corinne and Jared are having a great time with Fred and the bugs. A simple game becomes loads of fun when a goofy frog and a great mom join in.

You Will Need

6 green Connect-Its
1 pkg. Lace-Its
1 pkg. flower-shaped Button-Its
9" x 12" felt pieces, as follows:
- 2 white
- 1 blue
- 1 lime
- 1 green
- 1 yellow
- 1 pink
- 1 orange

3" square black felt
12" x 18" piece fun foam
3 oz. polyester fiberfill
36 black 4mm pompons
6 wiggly eyes
1 pkg. plastic pellets or rice
Fabric glue
Matching thread
Sewing machine
Upholstery thread
Needle
Embroidery needle
Scissors
Black fine marker
Disappearing marker
Pins
8 pattern pieces (#8)

Finished Size: 14" high and almost as round—oops!—square

tip

Reviewing Chapter 1 before you begin will be very helpful in making this toy. The chapter is filled with detailed information about all aspects of completing the toys. Specific sections are clearly titled for easy reference. Also refer to the pattern pieces for specific placement details.

Cutting Plan

1 Fred Frog is #8 on the pattern sheet. Using those pattern pieces, cut as follows:

- four feet from green felt
- four outer eye pieces from green felt
- six toes from orange felt
- 12 bug wings from white felt
- two inner eye pieces from white felt
- two bug body pieces from lime felt
- two bug body pieces from yellow felt
- two bug body pieces from blue felt
- two eye center pieces from black felt
- one mouth piece from pink felt
- one mouth piece from orange felt

2 Cut slits in two of the feet, as indicated on the pattern.

3 Cut slits in two outer eye pieces, as indicated on the pattern.

4 Cut slits in one of each of the body piece colors.

Making the Frog Body

1 Match one of the slit foot pieces to one of the regular foot pieces and sew around the foot with a ⅛" seam allowance. Repeat for the other foot. Turn both feet through the slits.

2 Glue the toes on the front of each foot, as shown at right, and let dry.

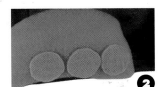

3 Stuff the feet with polyester fiberfill.

4 Sew the slit openings shut on the feet.

5 Glue each foot to the front of a Connect-It square and let dry.

6 Cut the lace into a length to work with and thread it through a needle or wrap the end with tape.

7 Place two Connect-It pieces side-by-side, and leaving the end of the lace extending 8", lace in and out through the holes down one side of the pieces, as shown. Leave the lace attached.

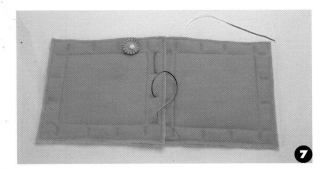

8 Put the bottom Connect-It piece into place and lace down one side of the bottom.

9 Go up between the next two sides. When the lacing piece gets short, leave it hanging at the closest end and begin with another piece, leaving the end hanging as on the first side.

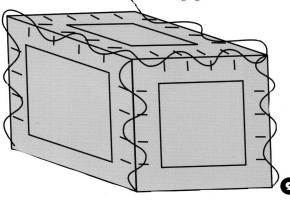

10 Tie the lace ends together where they meet, pull the lace tightly, and tie the other loose ends into knots.

11 Sew the knots to the inside edges with a needle and upholstery thread. Make several small stitches through the knot to hold it in place. Cut threads.

12 Insert fun foam inside the body to help it keep its shape.

Making the Frog Face

1 Trim ⅛" off all sides of the pink mouth piece. Center the pink piece on the orange mouth piece and glue in place.

2 Glue the mouth to the front of the body.

3 Insert the flower Button-Its through each of the top four corners for extra reinforcement.

4 With right sides together, match each of the slit outer eye pieces to each of the regular outer eye pieces and sew around the outer eye pairs with a ⅛" seam allowance. Turn each through the slits.

5 For each eye, glue the eye centers to the inner eyes and then glue the inner eyes to outer eye fronts. Let dry.

6 Glue the eyes together in the center of the head Connect-It piece, as shown.

6

7 Insert Button-Its in the front corner holes.

8 Fasten the other side of the Button-Its to the top of the body square at the back. Place the other two Button-Its into the holes on the top sides.

The finished frog opens wide, awaiting some yummy bugs to be tossed inside.

tip

To make the game easier, button the head close to the back, making the mouth very wide. To make the game a little more difficult, button the head in the center holes.

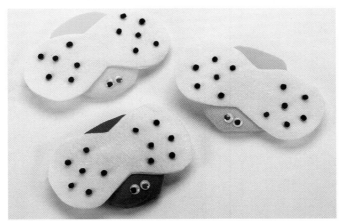

Try making bugs in several varying colors so that more than one can play.

Making the Bugs

1 Match up a slit bug piece to a regular bug piece of the same color and sew completely around with a ⅛" seam allowance. Turn through the slit. Do the same for each bug.

2 Stuff the bugs loosely with pellets or rice.

3 Sew the slit openings shut with upholstery thread and needle. This is the top of the bug.

4 Glue the eyes in place, as shown at right.

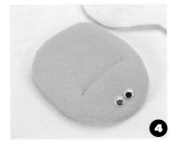

5 Glue six pompons on each wing for a total of 12 per wing piece.

6 Glue the wings over the slits on bodies for the finished bug, as shown at right.

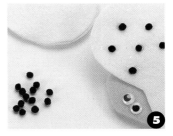

tip

Fred is a big frog so he has lots of room for bugs. Make a few more bugs to play with in other bright colors. Make sets of different colors for team playing. Spots on wings could vary for older children playing. They could add up the score of the bugs that end up inside Fred. Then, store the bugs in Fred when not playing with the game. That would make him very happy!

Tuttles Turtle

"T" is for turtle, tic-tac-toe, and a terrific good time. As far back as I can remember, I was playing the game and so did my girls. Such a simple game is ideal for a quiet playtime. Tuttles makes it extra fun with his shell being the playing board. The colorful pinwheel felt markers have a place to be stored inside. Abbie and Logan are playing the best out of three. Good luck!

You Will Need

⅓-yard lime felt
¼-yard green felt
9" x 12" pieces felt, as follows:
  • yellow
  • blue
24" length rickrack
6 oz. polyester stuffing
2 wiggly eyes
Fabric glue
Black dimensional paint
Matching thread
Upholstery thread
Sewing machine
Needle
Scissors
Black fine marker
Disappearing marker
Pins
4 pattern pieces (#9)

Finished Size: 14" long until he pulls his head in; he's a bit shorter then.

Cutting Plan

1 Tuttles is #9 on pattern sheet. Using those pattern pieces and making sure to place on the fold where indicated, cut as follows:

- two body pieces from lime felt
- one upper shell piece from green felt
- two under shell pieces from green felt
- one bottom piece from green felt

2 Cut the slit in one of the upper body pieces, as indicated on the pattern.

3 Cut rickrack into four 8" pieces.

> **tip**
>
> *Reviewing Chapter 1 before you begin will be very helpful in making this toy. The chapter is filled with detailed information about all aspects of completing the toys. Specific sections are clearly titled for easy reference. Also refer to the pattern pieces for specific placement details.*

> **tip**
>
> *When putting together pieces that have a narrow topstitch and curves, this method can make it easier.*
> *1. Cut two pieces of felt close to the pattern size.*
> *2. Use the marker to draw the pattern on the top piece of felt.*
> *3. Pin the pieces together inside the marked line.*
> *4. Topstitch in ¼" from the black line.*
> *5. Trim the black line off.*
> *This technique, which is illustrated below, keeps the felt from shifting, especially around small curves.*

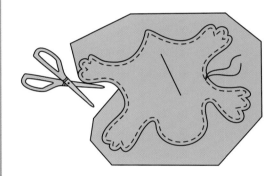

An alternative cutting and topstitching technique.

Making the Turtle

1 Place the body pieces together with the slit up, pin them together, and topstitch completely around with a ⅛" seam allowance.

2 Refer to the photo and pattern piece to draw on the mouth and toes with a marker first and then draw over the lines again with black paint. Let dry.

3 Glue the eyes in place.

4 Place the bottom shell pieces together, as shown, and topstitch with a ⅛" seam allowance, leaving an opening where indicated on the pattern.

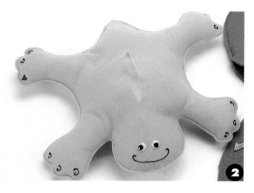

5 Glue rickrack to the top of the outer shell, as shown.

6 Sew the body slit shut with upholstery thread and needle.

7 Glue the under shell to the body and then glue the outer shell on top of that.

8 Turn Tuttles over and glue the bottom piece to the body, as shown below.

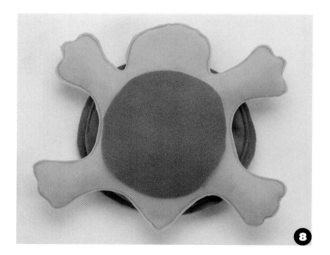

9 Cut 12 1" x 12" lengths of felt from contrasting colors.

10 Place two strips on top of each other and roll them up, as shown.

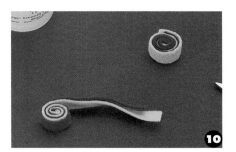

11 Glue the ends of the rolled pieces together. Lay flat to be used as marker.

12 Repeat steps 10 and 11 for the rest of the felt strips, making sure six of each are all the same.

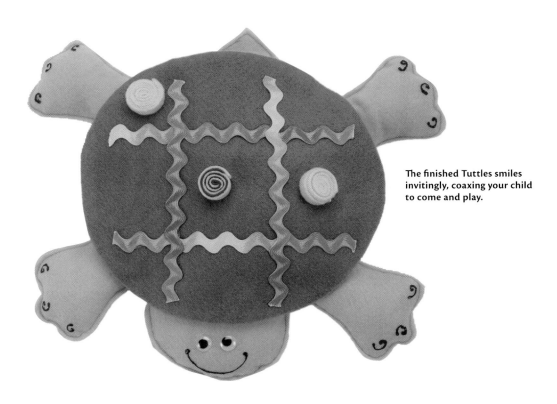

The finished Tuttles smiles invitingly, coaxing your child to come and play.

Butterfly Flower

Butterfly days are days of sunshine, flowers, and smiles. Sweet little Vanessa (whose name literally means "butterfly") sits among a happy flower and colorful ribbon butterflies. This matching game is full of color and results in smiles as bright as the sunshine needed to make your flower garden grow.

You Will Need

16" square fuchsia felt
16" square lime felt
9" x 12" pieces felt, as follows:
- one yellow
- one green
- one lavender
- one orange

6 oz. polyester stuffing
2 black 8mm eye beads
6 chenille stems, as follows:
- two orange
- two yellow
- two lime

3 yards 1½"-wide polka-dot ribbon
3 yards 2"-wide plaid ribbon
1 skein fuchsia floss
Fabric glue
Matching thread
Sewing machine
Needle
Wire cutters
Scissors
Fiskars Soft Grip scallop scissors
Black fine marker
Disappearing marker
Pins
5 pattern pieces (#10)

Finished Size: 15"

Cutting Plan

1. Butterfly is #10 on the pattern sheet. Using those pattern pieces and making sure to place on the fold where indicated, cut all pieces with the scallop scissors as follows:
   - one inner flower piece from fuchsia felt
   - two cheek pieces from fuchsia felt
   - one outer flower piece from lime felt
   - two face pieces from yellow felt
   - one bottom piece from green felt
   - one center piece from purple felt
   - one spiral piece each from lavender, lime, green, orange, fuchsia, and yellow felt

2. Cut slits in both the inner flower piece and one head piece, as indicated on the pattern.

Making the Flower Pillow

1. Draw the smile on the flower face with disappearing marker first and follow with two strands of embroidery floss and needle, sewing small in-and-out stitches along the smile line.

2. With upholstery thread and needle, sew the eye beads in place above the mouth.

3. Glue the cheeks in place for the finished look that is shown in the accompanying photo at right.

4. Place the two face pieces together, with the slit piece on the bottom. With matching thread, topstitch with a ⅛" seam allowance completely around the face, clip threads, and set the face aside for the moment.

5. With scallop scissors, cut along the lines on the spiral circles, keeping them in one continuous piece.

6. Glue one spiral on each of the six petals.

7　Place the flower bottom in the center of the outer flower piece, as shown, and topstitch with a ⅛" seam allowance around the center, leaving an opening, as indicated on the pattern. Repeat the topstitching again to reinforce the seam. Make sure to go back and forth over the end stitches to reinforce the opening.

8　Place the inner flower piece on top of the outer flower. Topstitch completely around with a ⅛" seam allowance.

9　Stuff the flower with fiberfill through the slit. Put small amounts of stuffing into the petals first, working towards the center.

10　With upholstery thread and needle, sew the opening shut, secure the threads, and cut the threads.

11　Stuff the face with fiberfill, pushing it to the edges of the curve to give a nice round shape.

12　Glue the flower center over the slit on the flower and then glue the face to the flower center on top.

The finished flower looks as sweet as a real flower smells.

Making the Butterflies

1　Cut ribbon into six 12" lengths.

2　Glue the ribbon ends together to form loops, as shown.

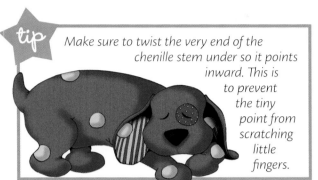

tip

Make sure to twist the very end of the chenille stem under so it points inward. This is to prevent the tiny point from scratching little fingers.

3 Twist two chenille stems together, as shown, varying the color combinations.

③

4 Place the narrow loops of ribbon on top of the wide loops.

5 Fold the chenille stems in half, place the ribbon loops in the center of the chenille, and pinch.

6 Twist the chenille halves together and roll the ends over a pen to make antennas for a finished butterfly, as shown.

⑥

7 Repeat steps 2 through 6 for all of the butterflies.

8 Place the butterflies in the pocket at the back of the flower pillow.

⑧

tip

Come and Play!
This is a game for one or more children to pull out butterflies from the pocket, one at a time. They match them in pairs by looking at the bodies. For younger children, the differences could be made easier by using different ribbons for part of the wings. Once the game is over and the butterflies are matched, just celebrate by tossing them in the air just like little Vanessa so happily did.

chapter 4

PUPPETS AND POPPETS

Imagination is a gift children have in abundance. A favorite soft toy is as real of a friend as a playmate who lives next door. Toys with personalities built in and lots of fun moves are sure to become a treasured friend. Sew a new friend or two—or more!—from this happy bunch of Bumbles Bunny, Leonardo Lion, Hamlet Hamster, Hocus P. Ocus, and Marvin Monkey.

Bumbles Bunny

Bumbles Bunny is my favorite toy in the book. I love many of them and like them all, but she is the one with whom the possibility of this book began. I have always had pet bunnies, and they have been a source of inspiration and fun. This cute puppet bunny hides in a lettuce head and pops out to surprise everyone with delight. Abbie just has to peek inside to find out.

Finished Size: 14" high (popped out) 10" high (hiding in the lettuce)

You Will Need

¼-yard white faux fur
½-yard lime speckled or
 flecked cotton fabric
¼-yard green felt
9" x 12" piece pink felt
¼-yard fusible interfacing
6 oz. polyester stuffing
4 yellow ¾" pompons
3 green ¾" pompons
2 10mm safety eyes
2 black 5mm beads
Fabric glue
1 skein pink embroidery floss
Matching thread
Upholstery thread
Sewing machine
Iron and board
Embroidery needle
Needle
Scissors
Black fine marker
Disappearing marker
Pins
7 pattern pieces (#11)

tip *Reviewing Chapter 1 before you begin will be very helpful in making this toy. The chapter is filled with detailed information about all aspects of completing the toys. Specific sections are clearly titled for easy reference. Also refer to the pattern pieces for specific placement details.*

Cutting Plan

1. Bumbles is #11 on the pattern sheet. Using those pattern pieces and paying special attention to those that need to be cut as reverse pieces (R) as well as those that are cut on the fold, cut as follows:

   - two head/body pieces from faux fur*
   - four outer ear pieces from faux fur*
   - one inside head lining piece from faux fur*
   - one nose piece from pink felt
   - two inner ear pieces from pink felt
   - six inner leaves from lime fabric
   - five outer leaves from lime fabric
   - 8" x 16" piece from lime fabric
   - two 8" circles (hat) from lime fabric (Use #10 Butterfly Flower bottom piece as your pattern for these circles.)
   - six inner leaves from green felt
   - five outer leaves from green felt

   * Be sure to place the nap of the fur towards you, wrong-side up.

Making the Lettuce Leaves

1. Following manufacturer's instructions, fuse the interfacing to the wrong sides of the fabric leaves.

2. Right sides together, sew all inner leaves to the contrasting inner leaves.

3. Right sides together, sew all outer leaves to the contrasting outer leaves.

4. Turn the ends in ¼" on the bottoms of all leaves, pin, and topstitch across all of the bottoms close to the edge.

5. Referring to the pattern piece for the pleat lines on the outer lines, fold the outer leaves, matching the lines. Alternate folding the leaves so three are folded one way and two are folded the opposite way. Pin, sew pleats, and clip all threads.

❺

6. Place the outer leaves side-by-side, alternating color. Overlap each side ¼". Topstitch along this line, which begins just below the curve. Leave flat.

❻

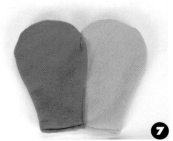

7. Repeat step 6 for the inner leaves.

❼

Making the Bunny

1. Referring to the head/body pattern piece, use the sharp point of scissors to make small holes for the eyes. Insert the safety eye ends through the holes and snap on the backs.

2. Glue on the nose below the eyes, referring to the step 3 photo for assistance, if necessary.

3. Thread embroidery needle with three strands of embroidery floss, knotting the end. Take the needle from the wrong side of the head piece just below the nose, make a ½" stitch straight down, and then take the needle through to the back again to create the finished mouth, as shown. Secure the floss with a knot and clip the excess floss.

4. With right sides together, place the head/body pieces together and sew around with an ⅛" seam allowance, leaving an opening at the bottom, as indicated on the pattern. Repeat the stitch around the piece again for extra durability. Clip the curves and the threads. Turn right-side out.

5. Place the inner ear pieces on the fronts of the outer ears, pin, and topstitch in place with an ⅛" seam allowance. Trim the threads.

6. With right sides together, sew around the ears with an ⅛" seam allowance, being sure to leave open the bottom, as indicated on the pattern. Clip the threads and turn right-side out.

7. With upholstery thread and needle, secure the thread at edge of an ear end. Sew around the ear with small stitches (sewing all the way around makes it gather tighter). Pull the stitches tight, secure the threads, and clip threads. Repeat this step for the second ear.

8. Stuff the head, leaving a small dent in the center of the stuffing for your fingers to fit in the next step.

9. Place glue around the wrong-side edge of the fur, inside the head lining. Insert into head to cover the stuffing. Press into the head.

10. With upholstery thread and needle, secure the thread to the ear mark on Bumbles' head. Sew through the end of one ear with the ear front down. Sew back and forth between the ear and head with small stitches. Secure the thread and then clip it. Repeat this step for second ear for the finished look shown in the accompanying photo.

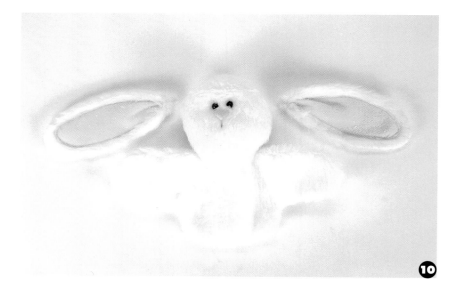

72

Adding the Hat

1. Cut 2" slit in the center of one hat circle.

2. Place the hat circles right sides together and sew completely around with ⅛" seam. Clip threads.

3. Turn hat through the slit, press, and then sew the slit shut with upholstery thread and needle, leaving the needle attached.

4. Glue the pompons together, alternating colors, for "Catypillar."

5. Glue the eye beads together on the first pompon.

6. Use needle and thread that is attached to back of hat to sew either end of Catypillar to the hat, as shown. Secure the thread at the back of hat with small stitches and clip the thread.

7. With upholstery thread and needle, sew around the hat with small stitches 1" in from edge, as shown, and leave the needle attached when finished.

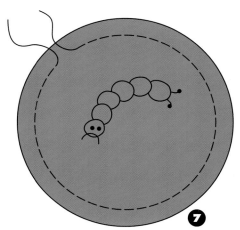

8. Put a small ball of stuffing in the center of hat and pull stitches to gather the hat around the stuffing.

9. Place the gathered hat on top of the bunny head to adjust gathers for a secure fit. Secure the threads with small stitches.

10. Continue with the needle through the head to the front of the hat on the stitch line. Take a small stitch. Go back and forth through the hat a couple of times. Secure threads at back of hat and clip thread.

Finishing the Lettuce

1. Press ¼" hem along 16" length of the 8" x 16" strip of lime fabric on both sides.

2. Sew small stitches along both sides, leaving the threads hanging.

3. Lay the fabric strip on top of the inner leaves strip, wrong side down.

4. Pull the stitches on the strip to fit the leaves, pin together the strip and the leaves, and topstitch across the bottom edge. Cut threads.

5. Place the outer leaves and inner leaves together, lining up the bottoms. The outer leaves are pinned to the opposite side.

6. With upholstery thread and needle, secure the thread at end of the leaves and sew across the bottom with small stitches through both layers of leaves. Secure and then clip the threads.

7. Fold the leaves with fabric right sides together and with ⅛" seam allowance, press the fabric seam flat and sew down. Turn right-side out. Clip the threads.

tip

The leaves with the pleats and the overlapped edges were too thick to sew both layers together on my machine. I found it was easier to sew by hand because of the thickness.

73

8 Center the seam at the back and insert the bunny body into the opposite end of fabric ½".

9 Pull the stitches to fit the body, pin in place, and with upholstery thread and needle, make small stitches around body, as shown. Repeat the stitch around for durability. Secure the thread at the back and clip the thread.

10 Fold the outer leaves back over the inner leaves.

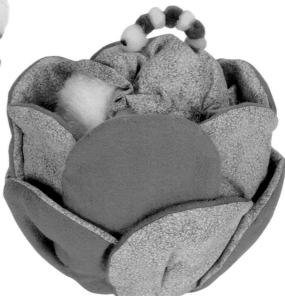

The finished Bumbles Bunny, which is shown above popped out and at right with the head pulled into the lettuce, is a cute and cuddly toy that is sure to befriend any little girl or boy.

Leonardo Lion

Who is hiding in the grass? Logan tries to see. It is Leonardo Lion, of course. Out he comes with a great big roar! This is a super-easy toy, but the ease in which it is made does not take away from its fun factor. His bright mouth opens wide to roar and roar and roar some more. The bright colors can't help but bring a smile. What a great puppet for a boy's safari-themed birthday party. Fill the house with a pride of lions!

You Will Need

12" x 16" yellow fleece
9" x 12" piece of fuchsia felt
1½" square scrap brown fleece or felt
1¾" square scrap orange fleece or felt
2 Connect-It!™ orange squares
14 Button-It!™ flowers
1 yard Chenille by the Inch™ Limeade
5 yards yellow Funky Fibers
2 15mm animal safety eyes
Fabric glue
Chenille Brush™
Chenille Cutting Guide™
Matching thread
Upholstery thread
Sewing machine
Iron and board
Needle
Scissors
Rotary cutter
Ruler
Spray bottle
Black fine marker
Disappearing marker
Pins
5 pattern pieces (#12)

Finished Size: 16" long

tip

Reviewing Chapter 1 before you begin will be very helpful in making this toy. The chapter is filled with detailed information about all aspects of completing the toys. Specific sections are clearly titled for easy reference. Also refer to the pattern pieces for specific placement details.

Cutting Plan

1. Leonardo is #12 on the pattern sheet. First prepare the head pattern to lightweight cardboard, extending the body 7" to either side.

2. Using the pattern pieces and paying special attention to those that need to be cut as reverse pieces (R) as well as those that are cut on the fold, cut as follows:
   - two body pieces from yellow fleece
   - four ear pieces from yellow fleece
   - two mouth pieces from fuchsia felt
   - one nose piece from brown felt
   - one upper nose piece from orange felt

3. From chenille strip, cut as follows:
   - two 7" pieces
   - two 5" pieces
   - two 4" pieces

4. Cut the fiber as follows:
   - 10 8"-long pieces
   - 10 7"-long pieces
   - five 6"-long pieces

Making the Body/Head

1. Referring to the pattern piece and picture in step 3, if necessary, make small holes for the eyes with a scissors. Insert the safety eyes and snap on the backs.

2. Glue the upper nose to the face, curving it slightly. Insert a tiny scrap piece of yellow fleece inside the upper nose and then glue the nose piece to the end of the upper nose.

3. Place the body pieces right sides together, pin, and sew the seams from the bottom up 8½", leaving the curved part of head unsewn. Repeat the stitch line for durability. Clip the threads.

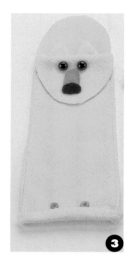

4. Sew the mouth pieces together, as shown, going over the stitch line a second time for durability. Clip the threads.

5. Place the ears right sides together, pin, and sew with a ¼" seam allowance. Clip the threads and turn each right-side out.

6. Press ends of ears together between your fingers, place glue on each ear end, and glue into position on the head as marked on the pattern piece.

7. With the body wrong-side out, pin the mouth into the head opening, as shown, and sew in place with an ⅛" seam allowance. Clip the threads.

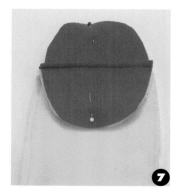

When pinning the mouth into the opening, you may find it does not fit exactly. No fear: There are two adjustments you can make. If the head opening is too large, sew the side seams up a little more. If the head opening is too small, open up the side seams slightly until the mouth fits.

Making the Bottom

1. Pin the chenille strips ½" apart to the front of one Connect-It!™ from long strip to short strip, as shown, and sew down the center of the strips. Clip the threads.

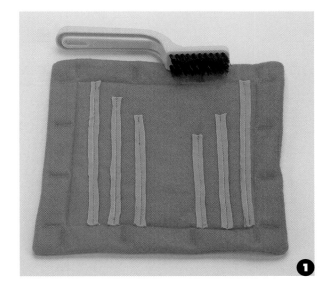

❶

8. Tie five varied lengths of fiber together by knotting them in the center, as shown. (Use two 8" pieces, two 7" pieces, and one 6" piece per bunch.) Tie four more bunches of fiber in the same manner.

❽

9. Secure the upholstery thread and needle at the top of the head, between the ears.

10. Insert the needle through the knot in one bunch of fibers and take small stitches at the head, pulling the fiber tight to the head. Repeat this step for the remaining four bunches, attaching them all between ears.

11. Secure the threads in the head with small stitches and cut the threads.

2. Spritz the chenille strips with water and brush the strips to fluff the chenille into "grass." Let dry.

3. Line up the bottom of the body with the holes on the Connect-It!™ square. Use scissors to make two holes in the bottom of body front and back to match up to the holes in the square.

4. With Button-It! buttons, fasten both Connect-It! squares together, as shown, along the two sides.

❹

5   Insert the body in between squares.

6   Button the lion body to the two center button holes, as shown, matching the front of the body to the front square and the back of the body to back of the square.

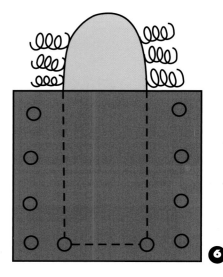

A fun and easy puppet, Leonardo Lion is a great toy for children to develop the fine motor skills of placing their hands inside and maneuvering the lion out of the grass.

7   Fold Leonardo down inside the square, as shown, and hand him over to a little lion tamer and watch for a roaring good time!

tip

This easy project can be made into all kinds of animals. Simply change the colors, nose, and ears by using other ears and noses from different projects in this book. Make a bear, a bunny, or a cat. Add button-on tails. There is no end to the animal parade!

Hamlet Hamster

A furry little hamster is often a first pet for many children. We have had many of them at our home. They are little escape artists, which aptly describes Hamlet. He is always trying to escape, but don't worry, just grab his tail and watch him bounce as he tries to get away. His jingly bell gives him away every time.

You Will Need

⅓-yard white fun fur
¼-yard tan faux fur
2 15mm animal safety eye beads
½-yard 1" print satin ribbon
2" jingle bell
Scrap brown fur
8 oz. polyester fiberfill
Fabric glue
18" pink embroidery floss
6" length ½"-wide elastic
Embroidery needle
Matching thread
Upholstery thread
Sewing machine
Iron and board
Needle
Scissors
Black fine marker
Disappearing marker
Pins
6 pattern pieces (#13)

Finished Size: 11" tall (and almost as round)

Reviewing Chapter 1 before you begin will be very helpful in making this toy. The chapter is filled with detailed information about all aspects of completing the toys. Specific sections are clearly titled for easy reference. Also refer to the pattern pieces for specific placement details.

Cutting Plan

1. Hamlet is # 13 on the pattern sheet. Using those pattern pieces and paying special attention to those that need to be cut as reverse pieces (R) as well as those that are cut on the fold, cut as follows:

   - two front/back body pieces from white fun fur*
   - one tail piece from white fun fur*
   - eight arm/foot pieces from white fun fur*
   - one contrast front piece from tan fur*
   - one contrast back piece from tan fur*
   - one nose piece from brown felt

   ✱*Be sure to place fur with the nap towards you, wrong-side up, and draw the pattern pieces on fur.*

2. Cut a slit as indicated on the pattern in white back body piece.

When working with fur, always cut through the backing only; do not cut the fur fibers. And when sewing seams, make sure to tuck the fur inside as you pin. If any fur does become caught in the seams, use a needle to pull it out. Sew the seams in the same direction, beginning at the center point on the rounded pieces and at the top on the straight pieces.

Creating the Face

1. With disappearing marker, draw a mouth line on the wrong side of the front head piece and mark eye placement.

2. Use the sharp point of the scissors to make holes for the eyes.

3. Insert the safety eyes through the holes and snap the backs onto the eyes, as shown.

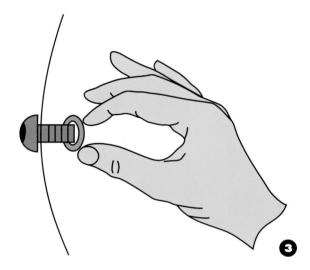

❸

4. Use three strands of floss with embroidery needle, knotting the end of the floss. Secure the floss on the wrong side of the front head piece in the center of the mouth, bringing the needle through to the right side of the face. Take the floss to right side of the mouth, going back through at the end of the mouth stitch, bring the floss and needle back through the center of mouth again, and then take the floss and needle to left side of mouth, going back through the mouth stitch. Secure the floss on the wrong side of the front head piece.

5. Glue the nose on the front of face, as shown.

❺

Making the Body

1. Place the front contrast piece on top of the front body piece with wrong sides down, pin, and topstitch in place close to edge all the way around. Clip the threads.

2. Place the feet and arm pieces right sides together, pin, and sew with ¼" seam allowance, making sure to leave an open area where indicated on the pattern. Clip the curves and turn each right-side out.

3. With upholstery thread and needle, sew the opening shut on the two feet only. Turn the opening in ¼" and pin.

4. Secure the thread at one side of a foot and take tiny stitches through both layers. Secure thread and clip.

5. Repeat steps 3 and 4 for the other foot.

6. Place the back contrast piece on top of the back with wrong sides down, as shown, and topstitch along the bottom only to hold the contrast piece in place.

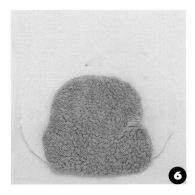

7. Pin the arms in place, facing them in on the front body piece.

8. Place the front body and back body pieces right sides together, pin-tucking the fur in as you go.

9. Beginning at the center of the head, sew with a ¼" seam around to the bottom. Sew the opposite side from the center of the head, overlapping at the stitches at the bottom. Repeat the stitch line for durability. Clip the curves and threads.

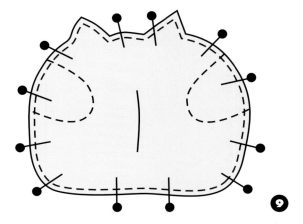

10. Turn the hamster body right-side out through the slit and fold the contrast back piece down.

11. Stuff the body with fiberfill through the slit.

12. Use upholstery thread and needle to sew the slit shut with small stitches.

13. Smooth the back contrast piece flat over the body back and then lift the back edges, glue, and press into place.

14. Put glue on the feet in 1" from the back of the feet and press the feet to bottom of body for the finished look, as shown. Let dry.

Attaching the Tail

1 Fold the tail in half with right sides together, pin the elastic at the top of the tail, as shown, and sew with a ¼" seam, catching the elastic in seam. Repeat the stitch line for durability and then sew over the elastic a couple more times for extra strength. Clip the threads.

2 Turn the tail right-side out.

3 Stretch the elastic from the inside to the bottom of the tail and pin.

4 With upholstery thread and needle, secure the thread at the elastic with several small stitches. Sew in and out around bottom of tail with small stitches. Pull stitches tight, leaving the thread and needle attached.

5 The tail is sewn to back of body just above contrast back, as shown. Sew from the tail to the body with several small stitches. Take a few more stitches to hold the thread securely. Cut the thread.

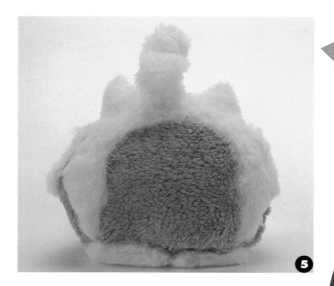

Adding the Bow

1 Slip the top of the bell through the ribbon and tie the ribbon into a bow.

2 Use upholstery thread and needle to sew the center of bow to front of Hamlet's body for a finished look, as shown. Sew on securely with several stitches.

tip *Vanessa is having fun with Hamlet. He bounces up and down when she shakes his tail, making him kind of like a furry yo-yo! Due to this heavy bouncing, he definitely needs his tail sewn on very securely.*

Hocus P. Ocus

Now you see him; now you don't! Magic is a wonderful part of life. You can't beat the surprise and the adventure of not knowing what might happen. Hocus P. is the tiny magician's assistant who waits in his hat to pop up as a delightful surprise. Logan had such fun with Hocus P., from popping the mouse up and down to putting the hat on his head.

Finished Size: 23" long

You Will Need

⅓-yard purple glitter felt
9" x 12" piece yellow glitter felt
9" x 12" piece black glitter felt
⅓-yard polka-dot purple fabric
5" x 15" piece gray plush felt
12" x 18" piece flexi-foam
2 yards ½"-wide yellow ribbon
6 yards ¼"-wide coordinating ribbons (1 yard each of six different colors)
2 black 6mm eye beads
3 glitter ½" pompons
½-yard ½"-wide elastic
1 oz. polyester stuffing
18" length 4" dowel
2" wood knob
½-yard red embroidery floss
Black dimensional fabric paint
Fabric glue
Matching thread
Upholstery thread
Sewing machine
Iron and board
Embroidery needle
Needle
Scissors
Fiskars Soft Grip Scallop Scissors
Black fine marker
Disappearing marker
Pins
8 pattern pieces (#14)

tip Reviewing Chapter 1 before you begin will be very helpful in making this toy. The chapter is filled with detailed information about all aspects of completing the toys. Specific sections are clearly titled for easy reference. Also refer to the pattern pieces for specific placement details.

Cutting Plan

1. Hocus P. is #14 on the pattern sheet. Using those pattern pieces and paying special attention to those that need to be cut as reverse pieces (R) as well as those that are cut on the fold, cut as follows:
   - two head pieces from gray plush felt
   - two ear pieces from gray plush felt
   - three stars (one each of three sizes) from yellow felt
   - one large hat piece from foam
   - one large hat piece from purple glitter felt
   - two mini hat pieces from black glitter felt
   - 10" x 20" skirt strip from polka dot fabric

2. With the scallop scissors, cut as follows:
   - one collar piece from yellow felt
   - 4" x 15" hat band strip from purple glitter felt

Making the Magical Mouse

1. With black paint, draw the swirls on stars, as indicated on the pattern. Set aside to dry.

2. Glue a pompon on either end of the collar, as shown. Set aside.

3. Press ¼" along one short side of the skirt piece and then press 1" hem along one side. Sew ¾" from fold to create the casing.

4. Slip the elastic through the casing, leaving the ends hanging. Set aside.

5. Glue the wood ball to the end of the dowel.

6. Beginning at the ball, glue ribbon end at an angle and wrap the ribbon around the pole, overlapping as you go, to the other end of pole. Glue end in place.

7. With right sides together, pin head pieces and sew with ⅛" seam allowance. Repeat the stitching for durability. Clip the curves and threads.

8. Turn the head right-side out and stuff firmly. (Plush has a slight stretch and will round out to a nice shape.)

9. Sew around bottom of the head with the upholstery thread and needle. Pull the stitches, leaving a hole for dowel to be inserted. Secure and clip the threads.

10. Secure upholstery thread and sculpture needle at bottom of head. Take the needle through the eye mark at the head front. Slide on a 6mm bead and take the needle back through to the bottom. Pull the thread to indent the bead into the face. Repeat this process for the second eye and then secure the thread at the bottom of the head.

11. With upholstery thread and needle, secure thread at bottom of the ear. Sew across the ear bottom with tiny stitches, pull the stitches tight, and secure.

12. Place the ears in position, standing straight out from head. Stitch the bottom of the ear in place with upholstery thread and needle. Stitch from the bottom of the ear to the head, using tiny stitches. Secure the threads with several tiny stitches together and cut threads. Repeat the process for the second ear.

13. Use three strands of floss with an embroidery needle, knotting the end of the floss. Secure the floss at the bottom of the head. Bring the needle through the head to the center of the mouth and then take the floss to the right side of mouth, going back through at the end of the mouth stitch. Bring the floss and needle back through the center of the mouth again and then take the floss and needle to the left side of mouth, going back through the mouth stitch. Secure the floss at bottom of head.

14. With right sides together, pin the mini hat pieces, sew with ⅛" seams, and clip the threads. Turn the hat right-side out.

15. Glue pompon nose on the face and glue the smallest star to front of the mini hat.

16. Insert the dowel 1" into head, pull it out temporarily, squirt in a good amount of glue, and reinsert the dowel.

17. Place the hat on the mouse head, gluing at the back by lifting the edge of hat slightly, placing a large dot of glue on the head, and pressing hat into dot of glue. Repeat for front of head for the finished look, as shown. Set aside.

Making the Wizard Hat

1 Lay the foam flat and then lay the raw edge of the fabric wrong-side down on long end of hat 1" over the end. Glue the fabric in place, as shown. Let dry.

2 Fold the hat band in half, wrong sides together, and topstitch along bottom.

3 Lay the felt hat piece on the foam, overlapping the skirt of the glued edge. Glue the felt to the foam hat all the way around the edges.

4 Glue the band along the wide end of the hat, scalloped edge down.

5 Fold the narrow end of the hat over 1½" and glue in place.

6 Fold the hat, overlapping the edges, as shown on pattern piece. Continue overlapping skirt also and glue in place.

7 Insert Hocus P. in through the hat, pull the elastic tight underneath the head, tie the elastic, and then cut the excess and tuck into casing. Place a little glue just under the head and push the casing into it.

8 Place the collar around the mouse neck and glue in place.

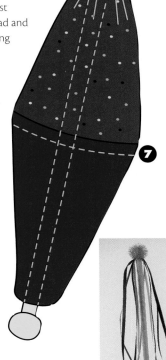

9 Glue the stars to front of hat, as shown, and tie the ribbons around the end of the ball by knotting them together at the center.

tip

This pop-up puppet and wizard's hat could be magically turned into a princess hat for a little girl. Make it from pretty pink felt and fabrics. Leave the hat off the mouse and add bows at the ears instead.

85

Marvin Monkey

Marvin just likes hanging around and grabbing for bunches of bananas. His arms and legs can be bent into different positions. He can hang here and there; he can hang from anywhere.

Finished Size: 20"

You Will Need

¼-yard cashmere tan plush felt
2 antique white 9" x 12" pieces felt
3 yellow 9" x 12" pieces felt
4 lime 9" x 12" pieces felt
1 yard 1½"-wide ribbon
2 black 8mm eye beads
8 oz. polyester stuffing
30" Chenille By The Inch™ Banana
Chenille Brush™
Chenille Cutting Guide™
8" length ½"-wide elastic
1 skein brown embroidery floss
Brown marker
Small round stencil brush or makeup sponge
Fabric glue
2 yards 26-gauge wire
Matching thread
Upholstery thread
Sewing machine
Embroidery needle
4" sculpture needle
Needle
Scissors
Rotary cutter
Wire cutters
Pliers
Spray bottle
Black fine marker
Disappearing marker
Pins
8 pattern pieces (#15)

tip

Reviewing Chapter 1 before you begin will be very helpful in making this toy. The chapter is filled with detailed information about all aspects of completing the toys. Specific sections are clearly titled for easy reference. Also refer to the pattern pieces for specific placement details.

Cutting Plan

1 Marvin is #15 on the pattern sheet. Using those pattern pieces and paying special attention to those that need to be cut as reverse pieces (R) as well as those that are cut on the fold, cut as follows:

- two body pieces from tan plush felt
- two head pieces from tan plush felt
- two tail pieces from tan plush felt
- four arm/leg pieces from tan plush felt
- two face pieces from antique white felt
- eight foot pieces from antique white felt
- four ear pieces from antique white felt
- three banana fronts from yellow felt*
- 3½" x 7½" piece from lime felt

❋*Do not cut the contrast banana backs yet.*

2 Using the rotary cutter and cutting guide, cut the chenille strips into six 5" pieces.

3 Cut the wire into four 10" pieces and one 14" piece.

Marvin Monkey has "bunches" of fun with his finished bananas.

Going Bananas

1 With the banana pattern piece as a guide, pin chenille strips to the bananas, sew into place and trim the threads.

2 Following the complete instructions on back of package, spritz a banana with water and brush the chenille strips until fluffy. Repeat for all of the bananas.

3 Pin a banana front to a piece of lime felt, as shown. Trim the lime felt to the rough outline of the banana front and topstitch close to the edge of the banana front. Repeat this step on the other two bananas.

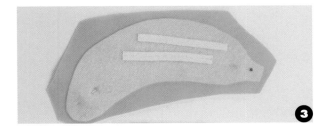

❸

4 Trim around the banana front, leaving ¼" lime edge all around. Repeat for each banana. Trim threads.

5 Cut a small center 2" slit through back of bananas only and stuff bananas softly with fiberfill.

6 With matching thread and needle, sew the slits shut. Secure thread at one end of slit and take tiny stitches back and forth across the slit. Pull stitches closed at end, secure the thread with several tiny stitches over each other, and clip threads.

7 Curve one end of the 3½" x 7½" banana stem piece and pin the elastic to stem piece, even with curved end 1" in from side, as shown. Sew the elastic in place.

8 Fold the stem piece felt in half, with the elastic to the outside. Sew along seam ⅛", clip threads, and turn right-side out.

9 Pull the elastic down to the bottom edge, pin, and topstitch across the bottom edge. Clip threads.

10 With upholstery thread and needle, sew bananas to the topstitched end of the stem. Secure the thread at the stem end with several small stitches. Take needle through the top of a banana and back through the stem. Place the next banana on top and go through the top of the stem. Repeat for the last banana. Stitch through them a couple of more times for durability. Secure the thread at the stem, taking several small stitches over the top of each other.

Making the Head

1 With right sides together, sew the head piece, face pieces, and ear pieces together. Repeat the stitching on each for durability. Clip the curves and threads and then turn each right-side out.

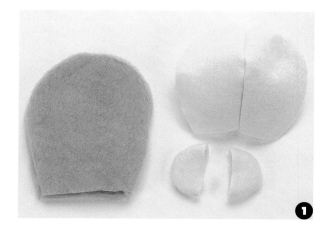

2 Stuff the head firmly. (Fur has a slight stretch and will round out to a nice shape.)

3 Sew around the bottom of the head with upholstery thread and a needle. Pull the stitches tight and secure and then clip the threads.

4 Center the face on the front side of the head, place a ball of stuffing under the face piece to fill out the center, and pin in place.

5 Remove the pins on one side of the face, lift up that edge, and glue along the edge. Press gently with your fingers. Repeat this step for the other side of the face.

6 Secure upholstery thread and sculpture needle at bottom of head. Take the needle through the eye mark at the face front, slide on a 8mm bead, and take the needle back through to the bottom. Pull the thread to indent the bead into the face. Repeat this process for the second eye. Secure the thread at the bottom of the head.

7 Bring the needle up through the head again to the nose mark. Take a small stitch and return to the bottom of the head. Repeat for the opposite nose mark. Secure threads at the bottom of the head and clip threads.

8 Secure three strands of brown floss and the embroidery needle at the bottom of the head. Take the needle up through the head to the eyebrow, as marked on pattern piece. Make a stitch and then take the needle back down to the bottom of head. Repeat for the second eyebrow. Return to the bottom of the head, leaving the needle and floss attached if there is some left. If not, secure a new length.

9 Take floss and needle out at one end of curved mouth stitch. Follow the dots to make the stitches to opposite side of mouth, as shown. Just take the needle in and out through the face piece only. At the opposite side of the mouth, bring the needle back through the stitches, filling in the spaces. Take one stitch to make a long stitch at either end of the mouth. Take the needle to the bottom of the head. Secure with small stitches and clip the thread.

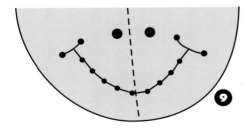

10 To add some shading to Marvin's face, use a stencil brush or sponge rubbed with a little bit of brown marker. Rub the brush on a piece of scrap paper first and then use a circular motion of the brush or sponge to shade around the eyes and nose, as shown.

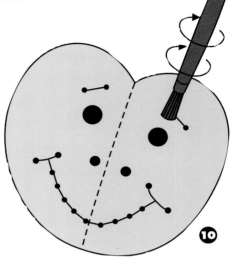

11 Glue the bottom of each ear together and then glue those bottom edges in a slightly curved position on head, as shown. Press with your fingers. Repeat this step for the other ear.

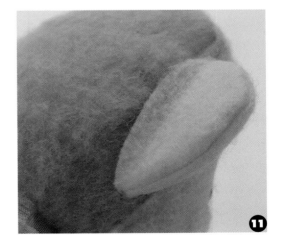

Making the Body

1. Bend ends of the cut wire pieces into small loops and twist them with pliers. To make sure there are no rough ends of wire, dab glue on the cut edges and let dry.

2. With right sides together, pin the arms, legs, and feet. Sew the seams on each and repeat the stitching for durability. Clip the curves and threads. Turn each right-side out.

3. Stuff all feet, making sure to push the stuffing into the thumbs first. Leave ½" empty at end on all four feet.

4. With right sides together, pin the tail and body pieces. Sew the seams on each, repeating the stitching for durability. Clip the curves. Turn each right-side out.

5. Stuff the body firmly.

6. With upholstery thread and needle, secure the thread at the top seam edge of the body. Sew around the top of the body with small stitches, pulling the stitches tight. Secure the thread with several small stitches on top of each other and clip thread.

7. Insert the wire into the arms and legs, pushing the loop to the "X" mark, as shown on pattern piece. With upholstery thread and needle take a few stitches through loop and both layers of each arm and leg to hold the wire in place. Repeat for both arms and legs. Clip threads.

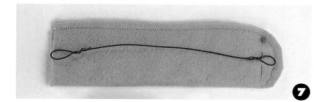

8. Secure the other end of the wire at the open end of each arm and leg by stitching against the center of one side of the limb. Repeat for both arms and legs.

9. Insert feet over the top of each arm and leg by ½". Line up the seams, fold the edges back, and glue. Press with your fingers. Repeat for both arms and legs. Let dry.

10. With upholstery thread and needle, secure the thread at the top of the body and alternate small stitches from the top of the body through bottom of the head in a 1½" circle. Leave the stitches loose until finished and then pull the stitches tight and secure the thread at the back of body. Clip threads.

11. Secure upholstery thread and needle at arm placement "X" on the body. Secure the thread with several small stitches and then take the needle through the "X" on one arm, back through arm, through the body, and to the "X" on the opposite arm. Repeat this step three or four times, returning the needle to the top of the body. Secure the thread under an arm and clip threads. Repeat this step for the legs.

The finished Marvin Monkey sits patiently awaiting a playmate.

12 Insert wire into the tail. With upholstery thread and needle, secure the loop at bottom of the tail to one side of the bottom edge. Take several small stitches to hold it in place.

13 Stuff the bottom half of the tail, lightly curving the wire into the center of the fiberfill. Leave ½" of tail empty at bottom.

14 Run a line of glue around inside bottom edge of tail. Press tail into place on body, as shown. Pin while drying.

chapter 5

TOPSY-TURVY AND A LITTLE GROOVY

These toys are just too wacky and loads of laughs. They twist, flip, or spin with the wildest hair imaginable. The joy of kids is that nothing is too silly and most often the sillier the better. This gang is super-silly and really groovy, sewn up in kids' favorite bright colors. Watch out for Willy Nilly, Hairy-Etta, Geeker, Raggle Taggle, and Pencil Poppers.

Willy Nilly

A silly little friend and his sneaker pencil case brighten up that special place set aside to do homework with all the necessary pencils, pens, erasers, and other little school supplies.

You Will Need

9" x 12" felt pieces, as follows:
- 1 yellow
- 2 peacock
- 2 baby blue

3 oz. polyester fiberfill

2 yards bright cording

6" x 2" piece red fun fur

2" hook-and-loop fastener

2 black 6mm beads

4 fuzzy ball ponytail elastics

Fabric glue

Black dimensional paint

Matching thread

Upholstery thread

Sewing machine

Iron and board

Needle

Scissors

Fiskars Soft Grip wave scissors

Disappearing marker

Pins

5 pattern pieces (#16)

Finished Size: 8" tall with 9" "sneaker"

Reviewing Chapter 1 before you begin will be very helpful in making this toy. The chapter is filled with detailed information about all aspects of completing the toys. Specific sections are clearly titled for easy reference. Also refer to the pattern pieces for specific placement details.

Cutting Plan

1   Willy is #16 on the pattern sheet. Using those pattern pieces and paying special attention to those that need to be cut as reverse pieces (R), cut as follows:
   - two sneaker pencil case pieces from peacock felt
   - two circle trim pieces from peacock felt
   - two sneaker upper trim pieces from baby blue felt
   - two sneaker sole pieces from baby blue felt
   - two body front/back pieces from yellow felt

Putting Willy Together

1   Place the two body pieces together and topstitch around them with ⅛" seam allowance, leaving an opening as marked at the top of the pattern piece.

2   Glue the eye beads in place, as shown.

3   Draw the mouth with disappearing marker and then paint along the mouth line, following marker line. Let dry.

4   Fold the long end of the fun fur strip over ½" and glue.

5   Stuff Willy by beginning in the end of the legs. Leave the top ½" of his head empty.

6   Glue the head opening shut by placing a line of glue along the top edge of the inside. Press sides together.

7   Begin at center back of head and wrap the fun fur hair around the head, bringing it to the center back again. Glue in place and cut off any excess.

8   Cut off the elastic loop from two of the ponytail balls. Glue the balls to the front end of each foot, as shown.

9   Pinch the other two ponytail elastics in half at their centers. Glue the center of each elastic together to create an arm with a ball hand.

10   Using upholstery thread and needle, secure the thread with small stitches at one "X" on the body. Take the needle through the end of one elastic arm and back through the body to the opposite side. Continue the needle through the second elastic arm at the "X" on the other side of the body and back through the body again. Repeat the back-and-forth stitching between the arms a couple of times.

11   Pull the thread tight to bring the arms snug to the body. Secure the thread with several small stitches just under the "X" on one side of the body.

Making the Sneaker Pencil Case

1   Pin sneaker upper trim and sole pieces to the back and front sneaker pieces. Topstitch with ⅛" seam allowance around each piece.

2   Cover the top of each piece of circle trim with a thin layer of glue and starting at the center, as shown, wind the cord into a coil to fully cover the circle. Press with your fingers to lay the coil flat. Trim off the excess coil and let dry.

3 Glue one piece of hook-and-loop tape to the inside top edge of each sneaker piece, as shown.

4 Cut one 18" piece of cord. Tie a knot at each end and then tie it into a bow.

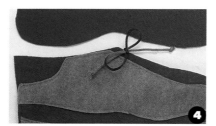

5 Place sneaker pieces together, right-side out. Topstitch around sneaker with ⅛" seam allowance, leaving an opening at the top, where indicated on the pattern. Stitch back and forth on either side of the opening to reinforce the edges.

6 Glue circle trim piece in place to front of sneaker and then glue the cord bow to top of sneaker for the finished look as shown.

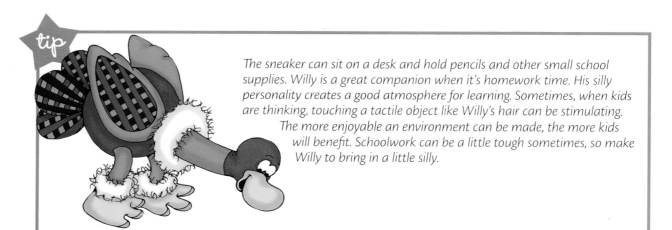

tip

The sneaker can sit on a desk and hold pencils and other small school supplies. Willy is a great companion when it's homework time. His silly personality creates a good atmosphere for learning. Sometimes, when kids are thinking, touching a tactile object like Willy's hair can be stimulating. The more enjoyable an environment can be made, the more kids will benefit. Schoolwork can be a little tough sometimes, so make Willy to bring in a little silly.

Hairy-Etta

Topsy-turvy dolls have been around for many years. Just like kids, the dolls can change from happy to grumpy or awake to sleeping. Hairy and Etta are always smiling, but like most girls, they want a different outfit and hairdo. They have gone a little overboard with having even their skin a different color. In any case, they are a delightful pair for a sweet little girl like Abbie to play with one way or the other!

Finished Size: 18" long either way (although Etta insists she is taller)

You Will Need

4 coordinating fat quarters (12" x 18"), one each as follows:
- stripe
- dot
- plaid
- small print

9" x 12" pieces felt, as follows:
- 2 fuchsia
- 2 yellow

6 oz. polyester fiberfill
2 black 8mm eye beads
2 8mm wiggly eyes
⅓-yard 1½"-wide coordinating ribbon
6 decorative ¼" buttons
4 pkg. decorative hair barrettes and
      elastics (30 to 36 pieces total)
Fabric glue
Matching thread
Upholstery thread
Sewing machine
Iron and board
Needle
Scissors
Black dimensional fabric paint
Black fine marker
Disappearing marker
Ruler
Pins
4 pattern pieces (#17)

Meet Hairy...

and this is Etta.

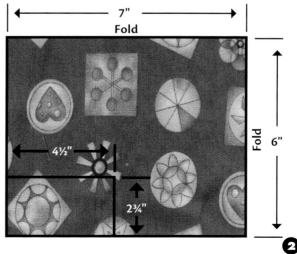

tip *Reviewing Chapter 1 before you begin will be very helpful in making this toy. The chapter is filled with detailed information about all aspects of completing the toys. Specific sections are clearly titled for easy reference. Also refer to the pattern pieces for specific placement details.*

Cutting Plan

1 Hairy-Etta is #17 on the pattern sheet. Using those pattern pieces and paying special attention to those that need to be cut as reverse pieces (R) as well as those that are cut on the fold, cut as follows:

- two skirt pieces from one of the coordinating fabrics
- two skirt pieces from a second of the coordinating fabrics
- two body pieces from fuchsia felt
- two contrast body pieces from yellow felt
- four hand pieces from fuchsia felt
- four contrast hand pieces from yellow felt
- two cheek pieces from fuchsia felt

2 Cut two blouses on the double-fold from the remaining two fabrics. Fold each piece into quarters with the wrong sides out. Pin the fabric along all four sides to keep it together. Following the accompanying diagram, use ruler to measure in 4½" and down 2¾" to create blouse piece. Draw along both lines with marker. Cut along those lines and discard the small pieces. Repeat this measure and cutting process for the second piece of fabric.

7"
Fold
4½"
2¾"
Fold
6"

❷

3 On one blouse piece, cut through one layer of the 6" fold to create the back opening and then cut ½" to either side of that opening at the top to make the neck opening. Repeat this step for the second blouse piece.

Making the Blouses and Skirts

1 Fold the blouses in half with right sides together and sew ¼" underarm seam along the cut lines on each side. Trim the corners and clip the threads.

2 Place the bottoms of the blouses right sides together and sew together, as shown. Clip the threads.

2 5

3 Press end of each sleeve under ½" and then press one side of the blouse back under ¼". Press all seams.

4 With right sides together, sew the skirt pieces along either side with ¼" seam allowance.

5 Pin the bottoms of the skirt pieces together, matching right sides. Sew with ¼" seam allowance. Clip at the corners and clip the threads. Lay flat.

6 Fold the narrow end of the skirts under ½". Press the folds and all seams flat as illustrated in the step 2 photo.

Creating the Bodies and Heads

1 Place the body pieces together and sew ⅛" seam around each body. Repeat the stitching line for durability.

2 Place the body pieces together at the bottom and sew one bottom section together, as shown, leaving the other open to turn body through.

3 Line up all hand pieces in pairs and sew together with ¼" seams, as shown. Repeat the stitching line for durability. Clip all threads.

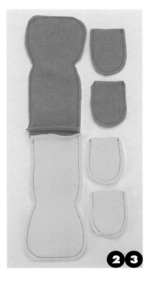

2 3

4 Turn body and hand pieces right sides out.

5 Create the faces by first gluing the eyes on and then drawing in mouths and eyelashes first with disappearing marker and then going over those lines with black paint, as in photos 5A and 5B. Glue the cheeks onto Etta's face, as in 5B. Let dry.

5A

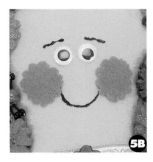
5B

6 Stuff the hands and bodies.

7 Sew the opening shut at end of the body with upholstery thread and needle.

"Dressing" the Dolls

1 Place a blouse piece on the body, overlap back seam, and glue or sew shut. Repeat this step with the other blouse piece on the other end of the doll.

2 Wrap ribbon around the neck, starting at neck seam, and glue in place. Repeat on the other neck.

3 Insert the hands into each sleeve end. Pin the hands in place, even with the inside folded line of fabric on each sleeve.

4 With upholstery thread and needle, secure the thread at the inside of each sleeve end ⅜" from end. Take small stitches through the sleeve and the end of the hand at the same time. Repeat for the remaining three hands.

5 Secure upholstery thread and needle at side of the head. Sew through the center of each hair loop, close together and one after another all around head. Repeat on the other head, as shown below.

6 Fasten barrettes into loops, as shown in the accompanying detail photos of each finished head above.

7 Fold one side of skirt inside the other, as though it were a lining.

8 With upholstery thread and needle, secure the thread at one side of the layered skirt top and sew small stitches around the skirt through both layers. Leave needle attached.

9 Place the skirt on the body where the blouse seam meets, pull the thread tight, and secure the threads with small stitches at the seam line.

 tip

Hairy-Etta is double the fun. She can spark imaginative play with conversations going on between the two ends and a cute little girl like Abbie. When she is tired of either Hairy or Etta, Abbie can just flip her. The flipping is fun, too, because her arms wave in the air.

Geeker

Just because you like doing homework and math puzzles that does not make you a geek. Then again, Geeker is a cool, blue dude with colored hair and lots of attitude. Let him hang out at your desk. He can hold some school stuff or secret snacks.

You Will Need

9" x 12" felt pieces, one each as follows:

- peacock
- orange
- white

2 bright 3" fabric scrap squares
2 bright 2" pompons or pompon hair elastics
2" x 4" scrap lime green polar fleece
3 oz. polyester fiberfill
4 black ¼" buttons
3 white ¼" buttons
Fabric glue
18" pink embroidery floss
Needle
Scissors
Disappearing marker
Pins
3 pattern pieces (#18)

Finished Size: 12" tall (if you include that wild hair!)

Cutting Plan

1. Geeker is #18 on pattern sheet. Using those pattern pieces and paying special attention to those that need to be cut as reverse pieces (R) as well as those that are cut on the fold, cut as follows:
   - one body piece from peacock felt
   - two arms from orange felt
   - two head pieces from white felt

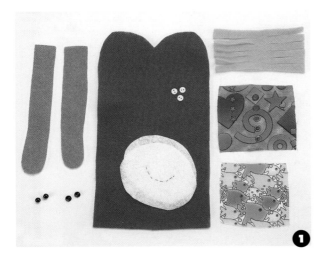

Making the Head

1. With the marker, draw in the mouth.

2. Use two strands of floss and needle to stitch the mouth. Knot the floss and begin at the back of one head piece. Take the needle in and out, making small stitches. Knot at back of head at other end of mouth.

3. Glue on the black buttons for eyes above the mouth.

4. Glue head pieces, wrong sides together. When dry, turn right-side out.

5. Fringe both ends of hair 1¾" on either side, leaving ½" in center, as shown. Tie the thread around the center of the hair piece tightly.

6. Place dot of glue at center of hair and glue to the top of the head.

Making the Body

1. Finger-press ¼" of fabric around all four sides of both pockets and glue the sides down.

2. Referring to the pattern, glue the pockets in place on the body.

3. Fold the body piece in half with right sides out.

4. Topstitch ⅛" from edge or glue along the inside edge of body, as marked on pattern. Let dry.

5. Angle the ends of the arms and glue an end of each arm even with the top of the body and side-by-side.

6 Glue the head over the top of the arms.

7 Glue pompons to the front of the bottom of the body, as shown, to serve as feet.

❼

8 Place the white buttons on the lower pocket and glue in place.

9 Referring to the accompanying photo of the finished Geeker, glue the end of the right hand to the mouth and glue end of left hand to upper pocket.

Finish front and back.

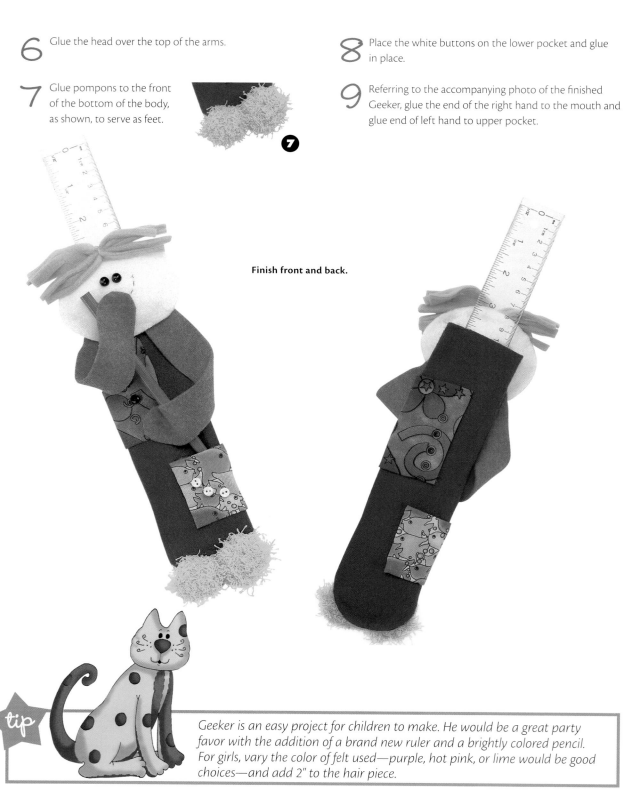

Geeker is an easy project for children to make. He would be a great party favor with the addition of a brand new ruler and a brightly colored pencil. For girls, vary the color of felt used—purple, hot pink, or lime would be good choices—and add 2" to the hair piece.

tip

Raggle Taggle

This is a lively character for sure. He is twice the fun with a wild personality on either side. Grab his braided arms and wind him up. Pull Raggle's arms out straight and watch him spin. Jared had a blast with this toy. Check out Lights, Camera, Action at the end of the book to see more fun shots with Jared. Raggle is so easy to make and definitely a boy's favorite kind of toy—action-packed!

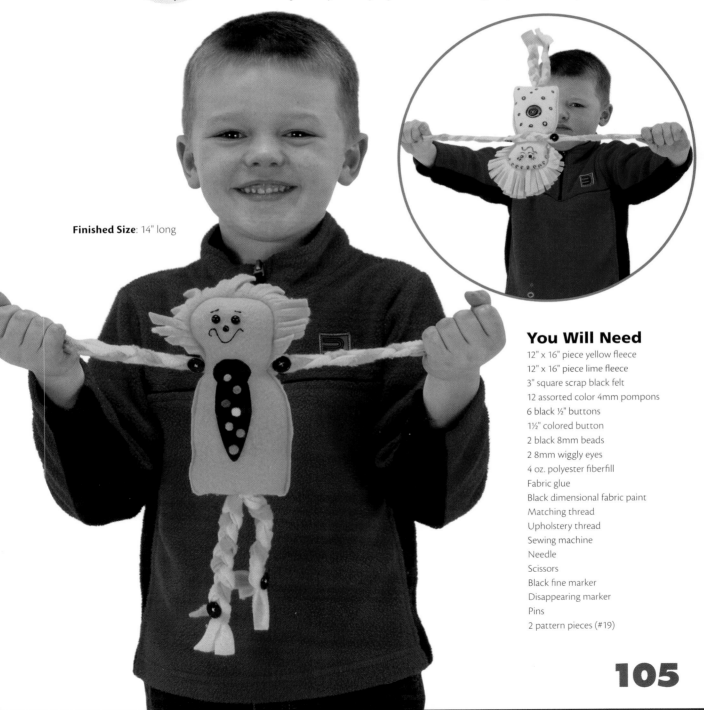

Finished Size: 14" long

You Will Need

12" x 16" piece yellow fleece
12" x 16" piece lime fleece
3" square scrap black felt
12 assorted color 4mm pompons
6 black ½" buttons
1½" colored button
2 black 8mm beads
2 8mm wiggly eyes
4 oz. polyester fiberfill
Fabric glue
Black dimensional fabric paint
Matching thread
Upholstery thread
Sewing machine
Needle
Scissors
Black fine marker
Disappearing marker
Pins
2 pattern pieces (#19)

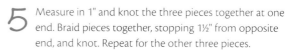

tip

Reviewing Chapter 1 before you begin will be very helpful in making this toy. The chapter is filled with detailed information about all aspects of completing the toys. Specific sections are clearly titled for easy reference. Also refer to the pattern pieces for specific placement details.

Cutting Plan

1   Raggle is #19 on pattern sheet. Using those pattern pieces and paying special attention to those that need to be cut as reverse pieces (R), cut as follows:
- one body piece from yellow fleece
- three 1" x 16" strips from yellow fleece
- one body piece from lime fleece
- three 1" x 16" strips from lime fleece
- one tie piece from black felt

Making One Side

1   With disappearing marker, draw the head/hair outline on the yellow body piece.

2   Place both body pieces wrong sides together and topstitch with ¼" seam along body and around the drawn head/hair line, leaving the bottom open as indicated on the pattern.

3   Make hair fringe by cutting with sharp scissors, as shown, along the lines marked on the pattern piece. Be careful not to cut through the stitching line. Stop short of line.

4   Place three 1" x 16" strips of fleece together—two yellow and one green. And then repeat, but this time with two green and one yellow.

5   Measure in 1" and knot the three pieces together at one end. Braid pieces together, stopping 1½" from opposite end, and knot. Repeat for the other three pieces.

6   Glue pompons to the felt tie and glue the tie to the body, as shown.

7   Create the face by first drawing the mouth and nose with disappearing marker and then going over those lines with paint. Glue on the eyes for the finished look as shown in the accompanying photo. Let this side of body dry.

Making the Other Side

1   Referring to the photo as guide, use disappearing marker to first draw in the facial features and swirls on body. Then, go over those lines with paint.

2   Glue eyes in place.

3   Glue button in place. Let this side dry.

Finishing It Up

1 Stuff the body.

2 With upholstery thread and needle, sew the bottom shut with tiny stitches. Secure and clip the threads.

3 Sew the black buttons at the opposite knotted ends of one braid, as shown. These are the feet.

3

4 Fold the buttoned braid in half and with upholstery thread and needle, sew the braid at the halfway point to the center of the body bottom. Sew over several times on the same stitch. Cut threads.

5 With upholstery thread and needle, secure the thread at one side of the body on seam. It should be just below hair fringe.

6 Center the second braid across the body, with arms extending evenly out to either side.

7 Take the needle and sew through the button on the braid. Then take the needle and thread through the body out to the braid and through the button. Go back through the button placed directly behind it on opposite side. Take needle back through body coming out on same side to go through button. Repeat by going back and forth through body and all four buttons.

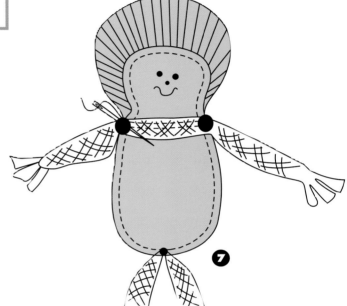

7

8 Secure the thread with several tiny stitches and clip the threads.

107

Pencil Poppers

These Pencil Poppers spin and jingle and bring on the sillies. Make a bunch with the kids and let them have a great time adding their own colorful accents. A wonderful party favor for all those birthday parties that come up. As you can see, Megan and Dylan have these little poppers moving at super-speed.

You Will Need (per popper)

6" x 10" scrap green or purple fleece
5" square felt scraps, as follows:
  - orange
  - peacock
½" pompon
2 10mm wiggly eyes
2 ½" jingle bells
2 18" pieces ribbon
Small clump fiberfill
Fabric glue
Matching thread
Sewing machine
Needle
Scissors
Black fine marker
Disappearing marker
Pins
3 pattern pieces (#20)

Finished Size: 10"

tip

Reviewing Chapter 1 before you begin will be very helpful in making this toy. The chapter is filled with detailed information about all aspects of completing the toys. Specific sections are clearly titled for easy reference. Also refer to the pattern pieces for specific placement details.

Cutting Plan

1 Pencil Popper is #20 on pattern sheet. Using those pattern pieces and paying special attention to those that need to be cut as reverse pieces (R), cut as follows:

- two ear pieces from orange felt
- two arm pieces from peacock felt
- two 6" squares from fleece

Making the Body

1 With a marker, draw the body pattern on one piece of fleece, as shown.

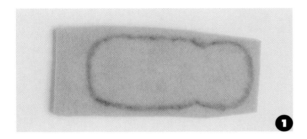

2 Sew around the piece with ⅛" seam, leaving an opening at bottom, as indicated on the pattern. Repeat the stitching line for durability. Clip threads.

3 Trim fleece edge close to the seam line and then turn right-side out.

4 Take the remaining piece of fleece and wrap it around the pencil, leaving 2" of pencil exposed at the bottom.

5 Trim off the excess fleece after overlapping it by ½".

6 Glue the fleece to the pencil.

7 Stuff the popper body two-thirds full.

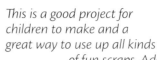

This is a good project for children to make and a great way to use up all kinds of fun scraps. Adding different eyes and using different colors can make their look totally different, as you can see in the accompanying photo. For a group of kids, get some colorful pencils, sew up a bunch of poppers and put out lots of scraps and snacks. You now have a cool party going on!

8 Insert body down over pencil and fleece, as shown, leaving 4" of the pencil exposed.

9 Squirt glue in the popper opening where it meets the pencil and press popper body to pencil. Let dry.

Finishing It Up

1 Glue on arms at "X" marks, as indicated on the body pattern.

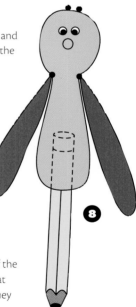

2 Place glue at the wider end of the ears and glue them together at the top of the head so that they are standing straight up.

3 Glue on wiggly eyes and pompon nose.

4 Tie ribbons together around neck. Tie a knot in the bow to keep it secure.

5 Slide bells onto the ribbon ends. Tie double—or triple—knots in the ends of the ribbon to keep the bells from shaking off.

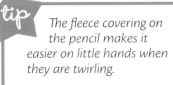

The fleece covering on the pencil makes it easier on little hands when they are twirling.

109

chapter 6

BEARS, HARES, AND HUGS TO SHARE

t the end of every day, there should be a special friend waiting for a child to share quiet moments with. These fuzzy, furry friends are perfect companions for any child. Sew up a special buddy who can be ready for lots of hugs, cuddles, and bedtime chats. This cuddly group, made up of Ted ZZZ Bear, Wibbit Wabbit, Dudz Bear, Wibbles, and Glam Bear, is waiting for a home.

Ted ZZZ Bear

The saying that a picture is worth a thousand words is true. Little Charlie with his blanket and Ted ZZZ brings many, many words to mind: precious, adorable, sweet. Ted ZZZ is a cuddly companion for bedtime and a great pajama bag during the day.

You Will Need

1 yard lilac fleece
⅓-yard white faux fur
6" x 15" teal fleece
⅓-yard print fabric
9" x 12" felt pieces, one each as follows:
- lavender
- black
- white
- brown

1 lb. polyester fiberfill
2 yellow 2" pompons
18" pink embroidery floss
Fabric glue
Matching thread
Upholstery thread
Sewing machine
Iron and board
Embroidery needle
Needle
Scissors
Black fine marker
Disappearing marker
Pins
13 pattern pieces (#21)

Finished Size: 30" tall

> ## tip
> *Reviewing Chapter 1 before you begin will be very helpful in making this toy. The chapter is filled with detailed information about all aspects of completing the toys. Specific sections are clearly titled for easy reference. Also refer to the pattern pieces for specific placement details.*

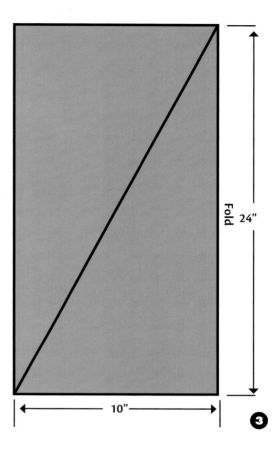

Cutting Plan

1   Ted ZZZ is #21 on pattern sheet. Using those pattern pieces and paying special attention to those that need to be cut as reverse pieces (R) as well as those that are cut on the fold, cut as follows:

- two body pieces from lilac fleece
- two pocket pieces from lilac fleece
- two head pieces from white faux fur
- two muzzle pieces from white faux fur
- two eyelids from white faux fur
- eight paw/foot pieces from white faux fur
- four sleeve pieces from print fabric
- two collar pieces from print fabric
- two outer eye pieces from brown felt
- two eyelash pieces from black felt
- two inner eye pieces from black felt
- one nose piece from lavender felt
- three "Z" pieces from lavender felt

2   Cut a slit in one of the muzzle pieces, as indicated on the pattern piece.

3   Cut the hat from lilac fleece by following the accompanying diagram and these simple steps:
   a. Fold piece of lilac fleece with right sides together to measure 10" x 24".
   b. Draw a line from the top inside point to the outside point at the bottom.
   c. Cut along this line, creating a triangle hat 20" x 24".

Fold

24"

10"

❸

Making the Hat

1   Fold up ½" along the 20" bottom of the hat and topstitch with ¼" seam.

2   Fold the hat with right sides together and sew ¼" seam along the cut line.

3   Clip threads and point and set the hat aside for the moment.

Making the Body and Head

1 Pin the paws to ends of the sleeves, right sides together. Tuck the fur to the front as you pin. Sew each paw to each sleeve with ¼" seams. Repeat the stitching line for durability. Trim threads.

2 Pin the sleeves to the body, right sides together. Sew with ¼" seams. Repeat the stitching line for durability.

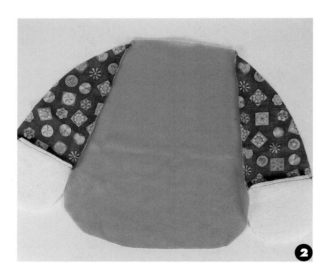

3 Fold pocket hemline under on both pieces and topstitch with ¼" seam.

4 Lay pocket pieces on top of back body piece, lining up the outside edges overlapping the pocket pieces. Pin overlap to hold it in place, as shown.

5 Pin the feet to the bottom of the body, side-by-side, as shown, with right sides together.

6 Pin the feet to the front of the body, making sure that the back and front feet match up. Sew with ¼" seams. Repeat the stitching line for durability. Clip threads.

7 Pin the head pieces to the top of the body pieces with right sides together. Sew with ¼" seam for the front of the head piece only. Leave the back head piece pinned in place.

8 Place the back and front body-head pieces together. Pin, tucking the fur to the inside. Sew completely around with ¼" seam. Repeat the stitching line for durability. Clip curves. Remove all pins. The back of the head opening is for stuffing the bear.

Making the Face

1 Place the muzzle pieces with right sides together and pin them in place, tucking the fur to the inside. Sew with ¼" seam.

2 Turn the muzzle through the slit, stuff, and with upholstery thread and needle, sew the slit shut. Secure threads with several small stitches.

3 Referring to the head pattern piece, as well as the accompanying photo, for mouth placement, take two strands of floss and an embroidery needle and secure the floss at the back of the muzzle. Bring the needle from the back of the muzzle to the front through the dot on the face front.

4 Bring the needle back through the muzzle just above the bottom of the nose. Secure at the back of the muzzle with a few stitches.

5   Glue the muzzle to the face, referring to the head pattern for placement.

6   Glue the nose in place, again using the head pattern as a guide for placement.

7   Assemble the four pieces for each eye. Fringe the eyelashes with a sharp scissors.

8   Glue the inner eye to the outer eye, as shown. Repeat for the second eye.

9   Glue the eyelashes under eyelids, as shown.

Finishing It Up

1   Stuff Ted through opening in back of head. Begin with the feet, paws, and ears, working towards the center.

2   Sew the back of the head opening shut with embroidery floss and needle. Secure the thread with several stitches. Clip threads.

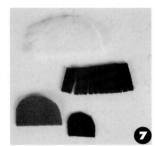

3   Place slipper pieces right sides together and sew with ¼" seams. Repeat stitching line for durability. Clip threads.

4   Turn the slippers right-side out and glue yellow pompons on the end of each slipper.

5   Stuff the slipper toes with polyester fiberfill.

6   Place the slippers over feet.

7   With upholstery thread and needle, sew the slippers to the feet with small stitches. Secure the thread with several small stitches placed together.

8   Place the hat on Ted ZZZ's head, grab a favorite storybook, and tuck everyone into bed.

10   Referring to the head pattern piece for eye placement, glue the eyes on first.

11   Place glue just around inside edge of the eyelids. Glue over the eyes, rounding slightly.

Wibbit Wabbit

Wibbit is my daughter Kate's favorite toy in this book. With her bright, sassy colors and stretchy limbs, Wibbit loves to dance and swing in the air. A flippy skirt and ears adorned with bright flowers make Wibbit Wabbit a lively pal to have around. Here, Megan and Wibbit have fun hanging out together.

You Will Need

⅓-yard pink fleece
⅓-yard yellow velour
1½ yards ¾" elastic
2 black 8mm eye beads
6 flower hair elastics
4 pink ½" buttons
3 yards sparkle fibers
8 oz. polyester fiberfill
1 skein yellow embroidery floss
Matching thread
Upholstery thread
Fabric glue
Sewing machine
Embroidery needle
4" sculpture needle
Needle
Scissors
Black fine marker
Disappearing marker
Pins
6 pattern pieces (#22)

Finished Size: 18" long (and so proud of her long limbs!)

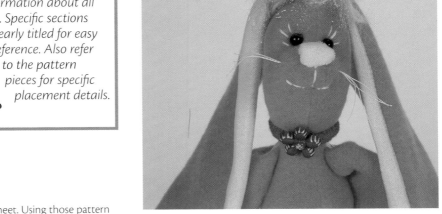

Wibbit Wabbit has a face any child could fall in love with.

Cutting Plan

1. Wibbit is #22 on the pattern sheet. Using those pattern pieces and paying special attention to those that need to be cut as reverse pieces (R) as well as those that are cut on the fold, cut as follows:
   - two body pieces from pink fleece
   - four arm/leg pieces from pink fleece
   - two outer ear pieces from pink fleece
   - two inner contrast ear pieces from yellow velour
   - four foot pieces from yellow velour
   - four paw pieces from yellow velour
   - one nose from yellow velour
   - 7" x 24" skirt piece from yellow velour

2. Cut the fibers into 12" lengths.

3. Cut the elastic in four 9" lengths.

Making the Body

1. Place the body pieces with right sides together, pin, and sew with ¼" seam, leaving an opening as indicated on the pattern. Repeat the stitching line for durability. Clip the threads and curves.

2. Turn the body right-side out and stuff it.

3. With upholstery thread and needle, sew the opening at the back of the body shut. Secure threads and clip.

Creating the Face

1. Use upholstery thread doubled and the soft sculpture needle to secure thread at back of the neck. (The collar will cover it.)

2. Take the needle through the head to the eye mark, as shown on pattern piece. Slide a bead on needle and take the needle back through the head, pulling the thread tight. Take a tiny stitch at back of head to hold the bead. Repeat this step for the other eye, making several small stitches together at the end to secure the thread and clip the ends.

3. With upholstery thread and needle, sew a small running stitch around the nose, close to the edge. Pull the stitches tight, creating a yo-yo. Secure the threads and clip them.

4. Glue nose in place.

5. Use three strands of yellow floss and needle and secure the thread at the back of the head. Bring the needle up as close to the eye bead as possible. Refer to lines on pattern piece for assistance. Make a stitch and take the needle back through head again. Repeat for the eyelashes on both eyes, returning to the back of the head.

6 Continue with needle and floss through the head to just under the nose. Follow the seam and take needle back through the head, as marked on pattern piece.

7 Come back through the head again to the outer end of one mouth stitch. Take the needle back through the end of the center stitch to the back of head, pulling the thread slightly. Repeat for the opposite side of the mouth. Secure the floss at the back of the head. Clip the threads.

8 Double-thread the sculpture needle with white upholstery thread. Take needle through the whisker dot and out again on the dot, as shown. Loop through the thread creating a knot.

9 Continue needle through head to opposite whisker dot, as shown. Pulling the thread tight, take a tiny stitch on the dot.

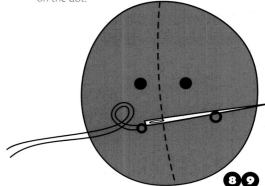

10 Clip the threads to 3" length or a whisker length of your choice.

Adding the Ears and Hair

1 With right sides together, sew the inner and outer ears together. Turn right-side out.

2 Turn the tops of the ears under ½". With upholstery thread and needle, gather around top of the ear. Pull stitches tight and then take a couple small stitches to hold the thread. Leave the needle attached.

3 Sew the ear to ¼" from seam line at the top of the head. Secure the thread under the ear. Clip threads.

4 Repeat steps 1 through 3 for the second ear.

5 Loop three of the fiber lengths together in half and tie in the middle. Repeat for two more bunches.

6 Sew the tied fiber bunches with upholstery thread and needle to the space between ears. Secure the thread at seam line and take the needle through the knot tied in the fibers for each of the three bunches.

Adding the Arms and Legs

1 Place the arm and leg pieces, wrong sides up. Pin the elastic to each piece, matching bottom, as shown, and then sew along the elastic at the bottom. Sew over the elastic three times for extra strength.

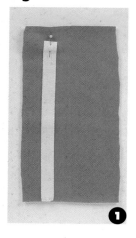

2 Stretch the elastic to the opposite end of the arm and leg length and sew into place. Sew over the elastic three times. Repeat for the other arm and legs.

3 Fold the arms and legs in half with right sides together and sew ¼" seam. Repeat the stitching line for durability.

4 With right sides together, sew the paws and feet in pairs. Trim curves and then turn each right-side out.

5 Stuff the paws and feet, leaving ¼" at the top of each empty.

6 Turn the top of each paw and leg under ¼".

7 For the arms, center the seam at the back, insert the end of an arm into the paw ½", and pin, as shown at right.

8 With upholstery thread and needle, secure the thread at the center back of the paw.

9 Make tiny stitches through the arm and paw along edge. Repeat the stitching for durability.

10 Secure the threads with several tiny stitches in one spot.

11 Repeat steps 8 through 10 for the second arm and both legs.

12 With upholstery thread and needle, gather around the top of an arm with small stitches. Pull the stitches tight, secure the threads, and clip the threads. Repeat this step for the other arm and both legs.

13 With upholstery thread and soft sculpture needle, secure the thread on the body at one arm "X" mark. With the seam on the arm to the inside, take the needle through arm, through the button, back through both, and through the body to the opposite arm and button. Repeat the stitching path a couple of times. Secure the threads under one arm with tiny stitches and clip the threads.

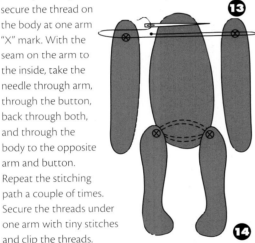

14 Repeat step 13 for the legs, making sure the feet face forward, for the finished look shown in the accompanying photo. (I have sewn a couple of animals that ended up walking backwards!)

Close-up of button-jointed arms and legs.

15 Slide elastics onto the arms and legs and also slide flower elastics over the head for around the waist and neck.

Making the Skirt

1 Finger-press 1" hem along the top of the skirt piece. Sew ⅛" from the raw edge to form casing for the elastic.

2 Fold the skirt in half with right sides together. Sew the back seam to the casing. Clip the threads and turn right-side out.

3 Insert the elastic through the casing.

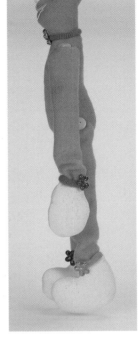

Side view of Wibbit Wabbit completed.

4 Place the skirt on Wibbit. Move waist elastic up out of the way.

5 Pull the skirt elastic tight, tie it in a knot, clip the ends, and tuck the knot inside the casing.

6 Slide the waist elastic back over the top of the skirt.

tips
• Wibbit can be hung around things by looping elastics into each other. I do not advocate putting things around a child's neck normally, but it does make a very cute picture with Megan. Wibbit is very stretchy and loose so she can't go tight around a neck. She loves to hang from desks and chairs, too.
• Make a boy version in bright blue—without the skirt, of course!

Dudz Bear

Who is the cool dude on the block? That would be Dudz Bear with his denim pocket sweatshirt and trendy sneakers. Dudz has all kinds of buttons and a pocketful of letters so every bear can be personalized. He makes for a good learning tool for spelling and word games. Plus, he's a cool companion for any little guy.

Finished Size: 20" sitting

You Will Need

22" x 24" red fleece
⅓-yard cashmere tan plush fleece
9" x 12" black felt piece
1 lb. polyester fiberfill
1 pair toddler white socks
1 pair size 5 or 6 toddler sneakers
Denim pocket from child's jeans
14 colored ½" buttons
1 skein black embroidery floss
1 pkg. felt letters
Fabric glue
White fabric paint
Matching thread
Upholstery thread
Sewing machine
Iron and board
Embroidery needle
Needle
Scissors
Black fine marker
Disappearing marker
Pins
5 pattern pieces (#23)

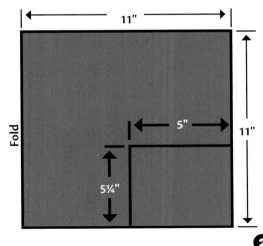

tip *Reviewing Chapter 1 before you begin will be very helpful in making this toy. The chapter is filled with detailed information about all aspects of completing the toys. Specific sections are clearly titled for easy reference. Also refer to the pattern pieces for specific placement details.*

Cutting Plan

1 Dudz is #23 on the pattern sheet. Using those pattern pieces and paying special attention to those that need to be cut as reverse pieces (R) as well as those that are cut on the fold, cut as follows:

- two head pieces from tan plush fleece*
- two body/leg pieces from tan plush fleece*
- four ear pieces from tan plush fleece*
- four arm pieces from tan plush fleece*
- two eye pieces from black felt
- one nose piece from black felt

* Be sure to place the plush fleece with the nap towards you.

2 Referring to the shirt-cutting diagram, cut the shirt on the double-fold from red fleece by following these simple steps:

    a. Fold the piece in quarters with wrong sides out.

    b. Pin the fabric along all four sides to keep it together.

    c. Measure in 5¼" with ruler and down 5" to create shirt piece. Draw along both lines with marker.

    d. Cut along the lines and discard small pieces.

| 11" |
| Fold |
| 5" |
| 11" |
| 5¼" |

2

3 Set the shirt, body, and arm pieces aside for the moment.

Close-up of finished head and face.

Making the Head and Face

1 With right sides together, sew the head and ear pieces with ¼" seams. Repeat stitching for durability. Clip the curves and threads.

2 Turn right-side out and stuff the head firmly. (Plush has a slight stretch and will round out to a nice shape.)

3 Sew around the bottom of the head with upholstery thread and needle. Pull the stitches tight and secure and clip the threads.

4 With white paint, dot the eyes. Let dry.

5 Referring to pattern piece and the photo that began this section, glue the nose and eyes in place.

6 Pin the bottom of the ears together and place in position. Stitch the bottom of each ear in place with upholstery thread and needle. Stitch from the back of the ear through both layers and into the head. Use tiny stitches. Secure threads with several tiny stitches close together and cut threads.

7 Thread sculpture needle with three strands of floss and secure at the bottom of the head. Bring the needle out at the eyebrow mark, as indicated on the pattern piece. Make a stitch and take the needle back through the head again to the bottom. Repeat for the other brow, returning to bottom of head.

8 Continue with needle and floss through the head to just under nose. Follow the seam and make a stitch. Take needle back through the head, as marked on pattern piece.

9 Come back through the head again to the outer end of one mouth stitch. Take the needle back through the end of the center stitch to the bottom of the head, pulling the thread slightly. Repeat for the opposite side of the mouth. Secure the floss at bottom of head and clip threads.

10 Set the head aside for the moment.

Making the Body

1 With right sides together, sew body pieces together with ¼" seam allowance and do the same on the arm pieces. Repeat the stitching for durability. Clip the curves and threads.

2 Turn the body and arms right-side out. Refer to the placement lines when stuffing and stuff the feet and paws firmly to the first lines. Stuff the middle of the legs and rest of arms softly. This will enable them to bend. Stuff the rest of the body firmly.

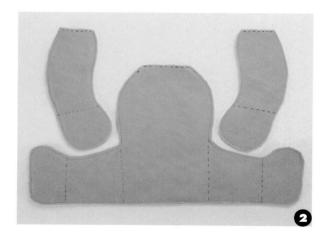

3 With upholstery thread and needle, sew around top of the body opening with small stitches. Pull the stitches tight. Secure the thread with small stitches.

4 With needle and thread still attached to the body, alternate small stitches from the top of the body through the bottom of head in a 1½" circle, as shown. Leave the stitches loose until finished and then pull the stitches tight and secure the thread with several small stitches close together. Cut the thread.

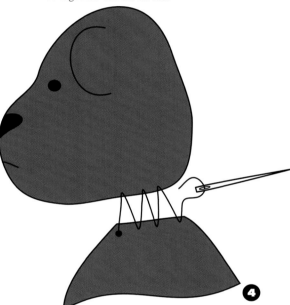

5 With upholstery thread and needle, sew around the top of the arm openings with small stitches. Pull the stitches tight. Secure the thread with small stitches close together.

6 With sculpture needle and upholstery thread, secure the thread at the "X" mark. Take the needle through arm at the "X," back through the arm, through the body, and to the opposite arm. Repeat this step three or four times, returning needle to the "X" on the body. Secure the thread on the body with several small stitches.

Adding the Shirt, Socks, and Shoes

1 With marker, draw a neck opening 1" x 3½" in the center of the red "sweatshirt." Fold under raw edge of neck, as shown, and glue.

tip

Not shown in photo is slit opening in back 3" in length. Fold the shirt in half lengthwise and cut the slit on the fold.

2 With upholstery thread and needle, sew three buttons that are spaced evenly along each shoulder, as shown.

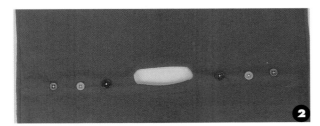

3 Sew buttons at each corner of denim pocket and then sew four more buttons in up-and-down positions spaced evenly across the pocket, as shown. (If you have a child's name with more than four letters, you will want to add more buttons to the pocket here and may even have to widen the pocket to allow them all to fit.)

4 Glue the pocket to the front of the shirt.

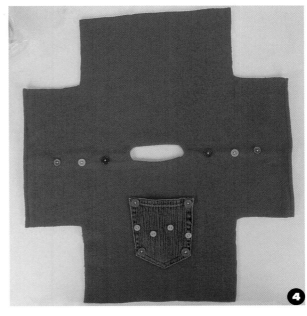

5 Fold shirt in half, matching the front and back with right sides together, as shown. Sew the underarm seams ¼". Clip curves.

6 Fold under ½" hem along the bottom of the shirt and sleeves. Topstitch each area with ⅛" seams. Clip threads.

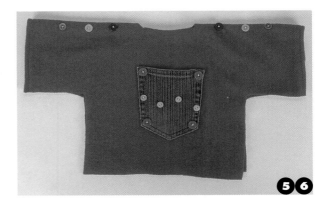

123

7 Place the shirt on the bear.

8 Fold under the edge of the back opening, overlapping the edges. With upholstery thread and needle, sew the opening shut, as shown.

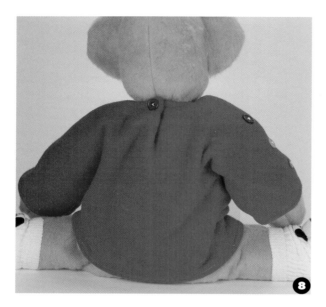

9 Cut tiny slits in the felt letters and fasten them to the buttons on the denim pocket. Place the rest of letters in the pocket.

10 Put the socks and then the sneakers on Dudz.

tip

My Dudz has very chubby feet. The sneakers I got on sale were a size 5 and so cute, but they would not fit over the socks. As always, there is a creative solution. I just cut off the bottom of the socks and tucked the top of the socks only into the sneakers. Too bad this little trick wouldn't work for kids since they are always outgrowing shoes.

Wibbles

Family is important, especially when it is a bunny family. There always seems to be lots of little bunnies around. Mama Wibbles has an easy way to carry her little family. She has a big secret pocket in her ear. The baby Wibbles can hop out anytime to play. They are bright and easy enough for the kids to make on their own.

You Will Need

½-yard fuchsia fleece
⅓-yard green fleece
½-yard coordinating print
9" x 12" felt pieces, one each as follows:
- black
- lime
- shocking pink
- orange
- white
- peacock
- yellow

4 10mm wiggly eyes
1 lb. polyester fiberfill
2 white 2" pompons
1 skein black embroidery floss
Fabric glue
Matching thread
Upholstery thread
Sewing machine
Iron and board
Embroidery needle
Needle
Scissors
Black fine marker
Disappearing marker
Pins
10 pattern pieces (#24)

Finished Size: Mama is 12" tall and her babies are each 4".

tip *Reviewing Chapter 1 before you begin will be very helpful in making this toy. The chapter is filled with detailed information about all aspects of completing the toys.*

Detail of Mama Wibbles' adorable face and head.

Cutting Plan

1 The Wibbles family are #24 on pattern sheets. Mama is on one sheet and the baby pattern is on the other. Using those pattern pieces and paying special attention to those that need to be cut as reverse pieces (R) as well as those that are cut on the fold, cut as follows:

- one Mama head piece from fuchsia fleece
- one Mama head piece from green fleece
- two Mama foot pieces from fuchsia fleece
- two Mama foot pieces from green fleece
- one 6" circle tail piece from green fleece
- two Mama ear pieces from fuchsia fleece
- two Mama ear pieces from print fabric
- one Mama pocket piece from print fabric
- one Mama nose from black felt
- two Mama inner eye pieces from black felt
- two Baby noses from black felt
- two Mama outer eye pieces from white felt
- two Mama eyelid pieces from lime felt
- two Baby ear pieces from lime felt
- two Baby body pieces from shocking pink felt
- two Baby body pieces from peacock felt
- two Baby ear pieces from orange felt
- eight Baby foot pieces from yellow felt

tip *For the babies, the pattern pieces give the pieces required for one baby. Depending on how many you want to make, just increase the number of pieces cut as we did in the Cutting Plan where the number of baby pieces is enough for two babies. The fun of the babies is to just mix up all kinds of fun colors of felt for their bodies, ears, and feet.*

Making Mama's Face and Head

1 Thread three strands of black embroidery floss on the needle, knot the end, and referring to the lines on the eyelid pattern piece, stitch, beginning on the inside at the top of the first line. Take the needle through to the front.

2 Place the floss on the first line. Take the floss and needle to the inside again and take the needle out through the top of the second line. Repeat stitch again and again until the last line is finished. Knot the floss on the inside of the last line.

3 Glue the inner eye onto the outer eye. Repeat for the second eye.

4 Referring to the pattern piece for placement, glue both eyes in place on the face front and glue the eyelids over the eyes.

5 Glue the nose in place.

6 Knot the floss again and take the needle through the face at the nose end. Make a 1½" stitch, taking the needle through to the back of the face. Knot the floss and clip the threads.

7 With right sides together, pin the Mama head pieces together and sew with ¼" seam, leaving an opening at the bottom where indicated on the pattern. Repeat the stitching for durability. Clip the curves and turn right-side out.

8 Stuff the head, pushing small amounts of fiberfill into the curves of the round body.

9 Turn the bottom opening of the head in and with upholstery thread and needle, sew the bottom shut. Secure and clip the thread. Set the head aside for the moment.

Adding Mama's Ears, Feet, and Tail

1 Press ¼" hem under on the pocket, then press under ½" again, and topstitch.

2 Place the pocket on one fabric ear inside piece with wrong sides together and pin. Treat this pocket ear as one piece.

3 Place the fleece outer ear pieces and fabric inner ear pieces together, pin, and sew the ears with ¼" seams. Turn each right-side out.

4 Place the feet bottom and tops with right sides together, pin, and sew with ¼" seams, leaving an opening where indicated on the pattern. Repeat the stitching line for durability. Clip the curves. Turn each foot right-side out.

5 Stuff the feet firmly.

6 Turn the foot opening ends in and sew them shut with upholstery thread and needle. Secure and clip the threads.

7 Turn the ends of the ears in ½". With upholstery thread and needle, sew around the top of one ear. Pull stitches to gather the ear to 2" wide at the top. Secure and clip the threads. Repeat this step for the second ear.

8 Place an ear in position on the head and with upholstery thread and needle, sew the ear to the head by anchoring the thread at one end of the ear and stitching in and out between the ear and the head with small stitches, as shown. Secure the thread at the opposite end of ear with several small stitches. Clip the thread. Repeat this step for the other ear.

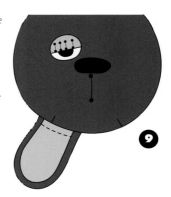

9 Measure in from the back of each foot 1". Place glue on this line and press the head bottom seam onto the line of glue on each foot, as shown at right.

10 Stitch around the edge of the tail circle with upholstery thread and needle. Pull stitches slightly to create a pocket shape.

11 Place a ball of stuffing in the pocket shape and then pull the stitches tight and secure the threads. Clip.

12 Glue the tail to the back of the head, just above the feet.

127

Making the Baby Wibbles

1 Glue the eyes and nose to the baby face.

Pieces assembled for baby construction.

2 With right sides together, sew the head pieces with ⅛" seam, leaving an opening at the bottom where indicated on the pattern.

3 Turn the head right-side out and stuff it.

4 Sew the bottom shut with upholstery thread and needle. Secure and clip the thread.

5 With three strands of black floss and the needle, bring needle from bottom of body to front of face just below nose. Make a stitch and return needle to bottom of face, as shown below. Secure thread at bottom of body.

6 Glue the foot pieces together in pairs. Place glue on the feet at marks, as shown, and glue side-by-side to the body.

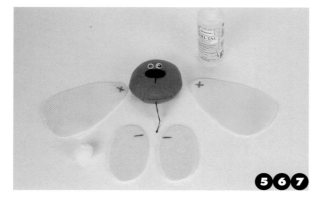

7 Place glue on "X" marks on ear pieces, as shown in the photo at the bottom of the first column, and then glue the ears to head.

8 Glue a pompon tail at head back, just above feet.

9 Repeat steps 1 through 8 for another baby in a different color.

10 Place babies in the ear pocket. Hop along and have some fun!

Glam Bear

Every little girl needs a soft companion to share giggly phone calls from friends or for those fun dress-up times and jewelry decisions. A girlfriend like Glam Bear is a must, as she is a dress-up diva herself. She always has a place for special treasures under her hat. It's really handy, especially if there are any sneaky little brothers around!

You Will Need

18" x 22" fuchsia fleece
¼-yard teddy brown tan faux fur
8" x 24" white faux fur
½-lb. polyester fiberfill
2 black 8mm beads
2 decorative buttons
1 skein black embroidery floss
Fabric glue
Matching thread
Upholstery thread
Sewing machine
4" soft sculpture needle
Embroidery needle
Needle
Sharp scissors
Black fine marker
Disappearing marker
Pins
6 pattern pieces (#25)

Finished Size: 14" tall

Cutting Plan

1 Glam bear is #25 on the pattern sheet. Using those pattern pieces and paying special attention to those that need to be cut as reverse pieces (R) as well as those that are cut on the fold, cut as follows:

- two head pieces from brown faux fur*
- two body pieces from brown faux fur*
- four arm pieces from brown faux fur*
- four leg pieces from brown faux fur*
- four ear pieces from brown faux fur*
- two foot pads from brown faux fur*
- 7" x 11" hat pieces from white faux fur*
- 4" x 11" collar piece from white faux fur*

❋Draw bear pieces on the wrong side of the fur with marker, making sure to place the fur with the nap towards you. Cut pieces carefully with sharp scissors, cutting through back only.

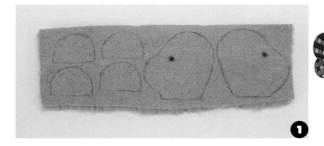

2 Referring to the cutting diagram below, cut the coat from fuchsia fleece on the double-fold, as follows:
   a. Fold the piece in quarters with wrong sides out.
   b. Pin the fabric along all four sides to keep it together.
   c. Measure in with ruler 4" and down 6" to create the coat piece.
   d. Draw along both lines with marker.
   e. Cut along the lines and discard the small pieces.

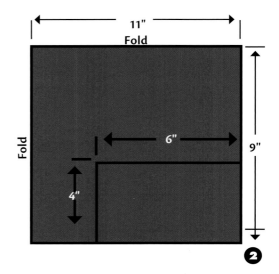

Creating the Head and Face

1. With right sides together, sew the head pieces together with a ¼" seam, leaving an opening as indicated on the pattern, and then sew the ear pieces in the same manner. Repeat the stitching line on each piece for durability. Clip the curves and threads.

2. Turn each piece right-side out and stuff the head firmly. (Fur has a slight stretch and will round out to a nice shape.)

3. Sew around the bottom opening of the head with upholstery thread and needle. Pull stitches tight. Secure and clip the threads.

4. Secure upholstery thread and anchor the sculpture needle at the bottom of the head. Take the needle through eye mark at the head front, slide on an 8mm bead, and then take the needle back through to the bottom, as shown. Pull the thread to indent the bead in the face. Repeat this process for the second eye and secure the thread at the bottom of the head.

5. Pin the bottom of the ears together and place into position on the head. Stitch the bottom of the ear in place with upholstery thread and needle by stitching from the back of ear through both layers and the head. Use tiny stitches. Secure the threads with several tiny stitches together and cut the threads. Repeat this step for second ear.

6. Trim the fur in the nose area. Secure three strands of floss and embroidery needle at bottom of head. Take the needle up through head to the nose as marked on pattern piece. Embroider the nose with a straight up and down satin stitch, as shown, and continue to create the mouth with a short ½" straight stitch below the nose and ½" stitch to the other side of the mouth. Secure the floss at bottom of the head. Clip the threads.

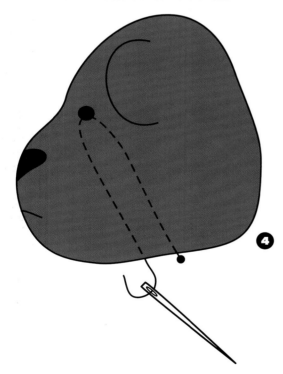

Making the Body

1   With right sides together, sew side body seams with ¼"
    seam allowance. Repeat stitching line for durability and
    then turn the piece right-side out.

2   With right sides together, sew the arm and leg
    pieces together, each with ¼" seam. Turn the arms
    right-side out.

3   Pin the foot pads in the bottom of the legs, matching
    dots indicated on the pattern pieces. Sew from "A" to "B"
    on either side. Clip the curves and turn each right-
    side out.

4   Stuff the feet and paws firmly, but stuff the remainder of
    the arms and legs softly.

5   With upholstery thread and needle, sew around top
    of the arm openings with small stitches. Pull the
    stitches tight and secure the thread with small stitches
    close together.

6   Center the seams of the legs, and with sculpture needle
    and upholstery thread, sew across the tops of the legs.

7   Turn bottom of body under ¼", insert the legs side-
    by-side into the bottom of the body ½", pin, and with
    upholstery thread and needle, sew the legs in place with
    tiny stitches back and forth between body and legs.

8   Take the needle through the top of one arm, back
    through the arm, through the body, and to the top of
    the opposite arm. Repeat this step three or four times,
    returning needle to top of body.

9   With the needle still attached to the body, alternate
    small stitches from the top of the body through the
    bottom of the head in a 1½" circle. Leave the stitches
    loose until finished and then pull the stitches tight and
    secure and clip the thread for the finished look, as shown
    in the two photos at the right.

Finished (but bare!) Glam Bear, front and back.

Isn't the finished Glam Bear just so glamorous, darling?

Making the Clothes

1 Use scissors to slit one fold of the coat for the front and then cut ½" on either side of the slit to create the neck opening.

2 Fold the coat in half, matching the front and back with right sides together. Sew under the arm seams ¼". Clip curves.

3 Fold under ½" hem along bottom of coat, coat fronts, and sleeves. Topstitch and clip the threads.

4 Fold up the hem on hat piece 1½" and glue. With upholstery thread and needle, stitch along the top of the hat, leaving the threads hanging, as shown.

5 Fold the hat in half with right sides together and sew the hat seam. Pull the threads left at the top of the hat tight. Secure and clip the threads.

6 Turn the hat right-side out and turn up the brim 1". Sew on a decorative button.

7 Place the coat on bear, overlap the front pieces, and sew on a decorative button to hold coat closed, as shown.

8 Fold the long sides of the collar under ½", glue, and then fold the collar in half with wrong sides together.

9 Wrap the collar around the neck, overlapping at the back. Trim off excess fabric and glue the ends together.

10 Place the hat on the head, but before doing so, tuck in a special gift to delight that special little girl.

133

MORE CREATIVE PLAY

You probably thought I was going to sleep through the whole book. I was just waiting until all my friends were ready to join me for some fun. Catastrophe and Wacky Wilma are my pals. We have some great ideas for play time. First, I want to tell you our story. Here goes ...

Stories and Ideas

Far away on a quiet road there lives a funny lady in a purple house. The windows have every color of the rainbow curtains blowing in the breeze. A big, cozy rocker that is draped with quilts sits on the front porch. Baskets of soft animals and bits and pieces of festive fabrics sit everywhere. A table nearby holds piles of papers with fun drawings of puppies and pigs and all kinds of things. Out comes the funny lady with the kind eyes followed by four cats, a big white dog, a little white dog, and a fluffy bunny. She sits in the rocker and begins to sew. The animals all go out in the yard to play.

Soon a black-and-white truck with red wheels pulls into the driveway and out jumps a dog, a cat, a guinea pig, and another funny lady with a happy smile. All the animals play in the yard while the two funny ladies sit sewing, drawing, and laughing all day long. They never forget the secret to a happy life is to follow your heart and work will always be play.

That is how we came to be. From bits and pieces of fabric, we were sewn with joy and stuffed with love.

Come follow us now as we have lots of ideas for you to play with us. Now I must be quiet for a bit because Catastrophe wants his turn to talk.

Counting Spots

Finally, I get a chance. Polkadilly is smart, but he likes to talk a little too much. He doesn't know everything. Take me, for example. When you make me, you could number my spots with felt numbers or paint and you could play connect-the-dots, I mean spots. Join spot 10 to spot two. I see some real twists and turns in my future. It'll be a good time counting for sure.

Fun Spelling

Then, there is our buddy Dudz the bear with the button-on letters. All kinds of words could be buttoned on. Cut out some simple shapes like a cat or dog and add the little slit. Button an animal on and spell out the word. Everything can be fun. Now there's a simple word—fun. All the shapes would go with that.

A Wibble Birthday

The Wibbles babies, like most bunny families, keep growing and growing. They are perfect for a birthday party as a favor. Write each child's name on an ear and place them at their seat. For children who are at least 7 or 8, they could each make one. Just sew the bodies on the machine and let the kids do the rest. Or pin up Mama Wibble, cut out of felt. Play pin the ears on the bunny. Have a wibble great time!

Fridge Bugs

Oh Ladybug's babies could really fly if they had magnets glued to them. They could be on the fridge ready to play a quick game after school. Oh Ladybug could use a babysitter sometimes.

Oh, someone is giving me the eye. I guess my turn is up. Wilma wants to squawk—um , I mean, talk now. Sorry, Wilma.

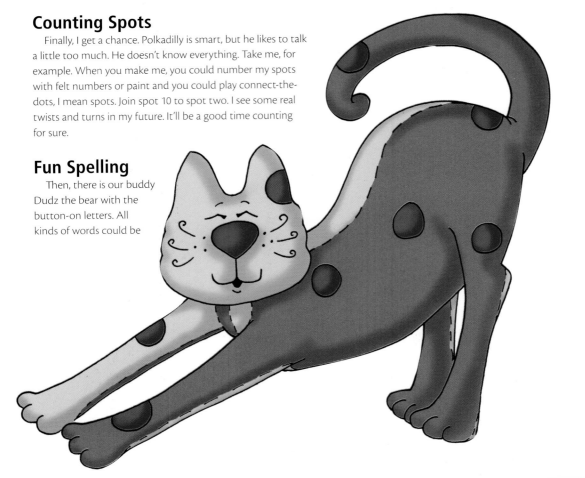

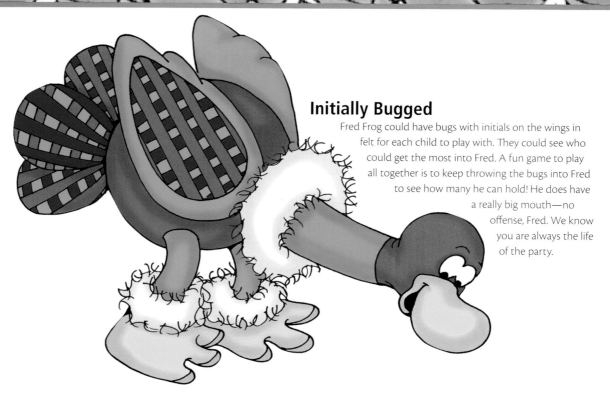

Initially Bugged

Fred Frog could have bugs with initials on the wings in felt for each child to play with. They could see who could get the most into Fred. A fun game to play all together is to keep throwing the bugs into Fred to see how many he can hold! He does have a really big mouth—no offense, Fred. We know you are always the life of the party.

Leo Transformed

It's about time. It isn't polite to keep a lady waiting. I have lots of good ideas. I can be a little wacky, but I am really smart, too. My mom always told me I couldn't always depend on my good looks.

Well, one of my best friends is Leonardo Lion. He thinks he is scary with that roar, but he only scares himself. He would have to grow a little more to be scary. Make his body in other colors, borrowing ears from another animal like Glam Bear. He could be a bear or a bunny or even a bird. Skip the ears on the bird though, pleeease.

Class Dismissed

The Pencil Poppers are perfect for the end-of-the-year surprises at school. Celebrate the last day with all the kids in the class getting them as a gift. The walls will be shaking once they get twirling.

Well, it's getting late, and I need my beauty sleep. Have a ball with all these fabulous ideas. Don't you think mine were fabulous Polkadilly?

Polkadilly?

Look at that, he is already asleep. Of course he does spend a lot of time sleeping. Did you see him in the rest of the book? Sleeping, sleeping, sleeping. I'm off to my feathered nest.

Remember each day to fill it with play!

Lights, Laughter, Action

The photo shoot for the book was a delightful, lively few days. The children ranged in age from almost 3 to 8 years old. Moms, dads , babies, aunts, brothers, and sisters also came along at different times, which contributed to the merriment. The children were engaging; a couple were shy but warmed up by the end. I brought storybooks and joke books and my beautiful voice (the dog likes it at home). It was an immersion in silliness as you can see.

Jared really got into swinging Raggle Taggle around and around and around.

Dylan gave us a smile, but we couldn't get Polkadilly awake long enough to give us one, too.

Charlie was the dearest little boy—utterly adorable in his pj's and carrying his blanket. Ted ZZZ is almost as big as he is.

Corinne and Jared enjoyed Fred Frog and the bugs. Corinne is one mom who doesn't mind a bug or two or three.

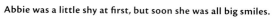

Abbie was a little shy at first, but soon she was all big smiles.

Watching Vanessa with Wacky Wilma was an enchanting delight. Wilma ended up with her feather boa just about everywhere except around her neck.

Megan and Dylan gave the Pencil Poppers a big whirl.

Logan was fascinated by Hocus P. Ocus. He even tried some magic of his own when he put on the hat!

139

Pattern Sheets Index and Project Numbers

Chapters are denoted by the symbols on the pattern sheets. Reverse each piece where indicated by (R) on the pattern sheet.

Chapter 2: Purrfect Pals and GRReat Buds

#1 Hot Dawg

#2 PeeWee Pup

#3 Catastrophe

#4 Polkadilly Pooch

#5 Skittles the Kitten

Chapter 3: Wiggles Jiggles and Lots of Giggles

#6 Wacky Wilma

#7 Oh Ladybug

#8 Fred Frog

#9 Tuttles Turtle

#10 Butterfly Flower

Chapter 4: Puppets and Poppets

#11 Bumbles Bunny

#12 Leonardo Lion

#13 Hamlet Hamster

#14 Hocus P. Ocus

#15 Marvin Monkey

Vanessa was getting a little tired and so was Hamlet. He didn't want to show his face to the camera at all!

Chapter 5: Topsy-Turvy and a Little Groovy

#16 Willy Nilly

#17 Hairy-Etta

#18 Geeker

#19 Raggle Taggle

#20 Pencil Poppers

Chapter 6: Bears, Hares and Hugs to Share

#21 Ted ZZZ Bear

#22 Wibbit Wabbit

#23 Dudz Bear

#24 Wibbles

#25 Glam Bear

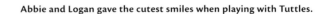

Abbie and Logan gave the cutest smiles when playing with Tuttles.

Source Information

Support your local craft and fabric retailers. If you are unable to find a particular product, contact the manufacturer to locate a store or mail-order source.

Beacon Chemical Company, Inc.
Fabri-Tac™ glue
(914) 699-3400

Coats & Clark
Embroidery floss, upholstery thread
(800) 648-1479

Colonial Needle Company
Sharps, soft sculpture, embroidery needles
(914) 237-6434

Daisy Kingdom
Connect-It!™
www.daisykingdom.com/craft

Fabric Cafe™
Chenille By The Inch™
www.fabriccafe.com

Fiskars
Softgrip wave and scallop scissors, Microtip Scissors, rotary cutters, self-healing mats, rulers.
www.fiskars.com

Lily Lake Crafts
Funky Fibers
www.lilylakecrafts.com

john bead corp. ltd.
Safety eyes, eye beads, chenille stems, variety of craft supplies
www.johnbead.com

Kunin Felt
Rainbow Classic Felt, Plush Felt, Glitter Felt, felt letters.
www.kuninfelt.com

Monterey, Inc.
www.montereyoutlet.com

Offray Ribbon
(800) 344-5533

Plaid
Dimensional Fabric Paint
www.plaidonline.com

About the Author

Debra Quartermain is a talented designer and author who delights in creating and sharing her whimsical designs. Her soft animals are found in magazines, books (including *Nursery Décor* published by KP Books in 2002), project sheets, and her own pattern line.

Debra has taught classes in sewing and crafting for many years. The last few years, teaching children has been her main focus in her spare time.

From childhood, Debra has always sewn and crafted, making doll clothes, her own clothes, and her children's clothes.

As a member of the Society of Craft Designers, she is involved in the creative industry, traveling to several tradeshows and seminars each year, as well as volunteering at these events.

"The craft industry is an exciting and supportive industry to be part of," she says. "Every day brings new opportunities and adventure. The creative life is a charmed one."

Debra lives in the small village of New Maryland in New Brunswick, Canada, with her two daughters, Amanda and Kate.

More Interactive* Fun
for the Little Ones in Your Life

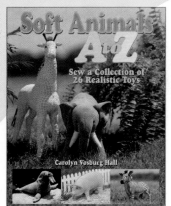

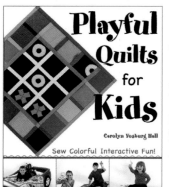
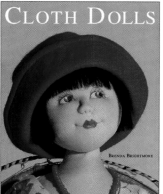
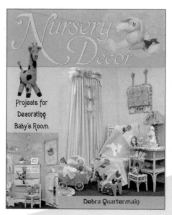